The GRILLING Bible

Publications International, Ltd.

Pictured on the front cover: Drunken T-Bone Steak *(page 40)*.

Pictured on the back cover *(top to bottom):* Caveman Beef Back Ribs *(page 22)*, Grilled Chicken with Chili Beer Baste *(page 164)* and Chili-Rubbed Grilled Vegetable Kabobs *(page 202)*.

ISBN: 978-1-4508-8364-1

Library of Congress Control Number: 2013952017

Manufactured in China.

8 7 6 5 4 3 2 1

Microwave Cooking: Microwave ovens vary in wattage. Use the cooking times as guidelines and check for doneness before adding more time.

Preparation/Cooking Times: Preparation times are based on the approximate amount of time required to assemble the recipe before cooking, baking, chilling or serving. These times include preparation steps such as measuring, chopping and mixing. The fact that some preparations and cooking can be done simultaneously is taken into account. Preparation of optional ingredients and serving suggestions is not included.

CONTENTS

Grilling Essentials

Few cooking methods compare to preparing food over flames. This tantalizing style of cooking with its mouthwatering aromas offers endless opportunities for both the novice and the pro. Fan the flames of your love of grilling with this versatile collection of recipes. And take a moment to review this section to brush up on some essentials.

CHOOSING A GRILL

Before you buy a grill, take some time to research the right grill for you. Consider where you grill, what you'll be cooking, the seasons when you'll be grilling and your budget. Choosing between a charcoal or gas grill is the biggest decision. Either will do an excellent job.

Charcoal grills generally burn hotter than gas grills. They're easier to use for smoking and there are those who think charcoal is the only way to get authentic grilled flavor.

Gas grills light instantly with the push of a button and offer steady heat that is easily adjusted. They make it easy to grill anything at any time.

CHARCOAL STARTING TIPS

For Safety's Sake

Make sure the grill is located outside on a solid surface, set away from shrubbery, grass and overhangs. Never light a grill inside or on a wooden deck.

• Make sure the grill vents are not clogged with ashes before starting a fire.
• Soak the coals with lighter fluid. Using gasoline, kerosene or paint thinner to start a charcoal fire can cause an explosion.
• Keep lighter fluid away from the fire. Do not add more lighter fluid to burning coals.
• Keep a water-filled spray bottle near the grill to quench flare-ups.

Number of Coals

The number of coals required for grilling depends on the size and type of grill, the amount of food to be prepared and weather conditions. As a general rule, it takes about 30 coals to grill one pound of meat under optimum weather conditions.

Starting the Coals

Make a Pyramid

To light a charcoal fire, arrange the coals in a pyramid shape about 20 to 30 minutes prior to cooking. The pyramid shape provides enough ventilation for the coals to catch fire. To start with lighter fluid, soak the coals with about ½ cup fluid. Wait one minute to allow the fluid to soak into the coals. Light with a match.

Electric Starter

To start with an electric starter, nestle the starter in the center of coals. Plug the starter into an outlet. After 8 to 10 minutes, when ash begins to form on the coals, unplug the starter and remove it.

Chimney Starter

To start with a chimney starter, remove the grid from the grill; place the chimney starter on the bottom rack. Crumple a few sheets of newspaper and place them in the bottom portion of the chimney starter. Fill the top portion with coals. Light the newspaper. Do not disturb the starter; the coals will be ready in 20 to 30 minutes. Be sure to wear fireproof mitts when pouring the hot coals from the chimney starter into the base of the grill.

The Coals Are Ready

When the coals are ready, they will be about 80 percent ash gray during daylight and will glow at night. Spread the coals in a single layer with long-handled tongs. To lower the cooking temperature, spread the coals farther apart or raise the grid. To raise the cooking temperature, either lower the grid or move the coals closer together and tap off the ash.

Checking Charcoal Temperature

A quick, easy way to estimate the temperature of the coals is to cautiously hold your hand, palm side down, about 4 inches above the coals. Count the number of seconds you can hold your hand in that position before the heat forces you to pull it away.

Seconds	Coal Temperature
2	hot (400°F or more)
3	medium-hot (350° to 375°F)
4	medium (300° to 350°F)
5	low (200° to 300°F)

USING A GAS GRILL

Follow the instructions in your owner's manual for lighting a gas grill. Once the grill is lit, turn all burners to HIGH about 10 minutes before cooking.

Gas grills cook the most evenly and with the fewest flare-ups at MEDIUM or LOW, with temperatures in the 250° to 375°F range. This is equivalent to medium-hot to low for charcoal.

Fire Safety

If flare-ups are a problem, one or more of the burners can be turned to a lower setting.

• Do not use water to quench flare-ups on a gas grill. Close the hood and turn the heat down until the flaring subsides.

• Trimming as much fat as possible from the meat before grilling or using a drip pan also helps.

FOOD SAFETY AND GRILLING

• Wash your hands often.
• Marinate safely.
• Keep raw foods separate from cooked foods.
• Use a clean plate when removing cooked food from the grill.
• Keep raw meats, poultry and fish in the refrigerator until ready to grill.

COOKING METHODS

There are two basic methods of cooking on a grill: direct and indirect.

Direct Grilling

Direct grilling means the food is placed right over the fire. It is best for smaller cuts of meat, fish and vegetables that can be cooked through in about 20 minutes. It's ideal for boneless chicken breasts, burgers, fish fillets, steaks, pork tenderloin and vegetables.

• **For direct cooking over charcoal,** place the food on the grid directly above the coals. Make sure there is enough charcoal in a single layer to extend 1 to 2 inches beyond the area of the food on the grill.

• **For direct cooking on a gas grill,** preheat the grill 10 to 15 minutes before you start cooking. Place the food on the grid and follow the cooking times in the recipe.

Indirect Grilling

Indirect grilling means the food is placed to the side of the fire. This method is best used for foods that require longer cooking time and less intense heat, such as roasts, whole chickens and turkeys and ribs.

• **For indirect cooking over charcoal,** place a foil drip pan on the bottom rack with the coals banked on both sides of the pan. Put the grid over both and place the food on the grid directly above the pan. When barbecuing by indirect cooking for more than 45 minutes, add 4 to 9 coals around the outer edge of the fire just before you begin grilling. When these coals are ready, add them to the center of the fire as needed to maintain a constant temperature.

• **For indirect cooking on a gas grill,** preheat the grill. Turn the center burner OFF and the two side burners to medium. Place a foil drip pan directly on the lava rocks in the center of the grill. Place the food on the grid directly above the drip pan. For a dual burner grill, turn one side of the grill OFF. Place the food on the unheated side of the grill, above the drip pan.

Sizzling Beef

Almost everyone loves the robust flavor of beef grilled outdoors. And, best of all, with tender steaks and burgers, you can have a complete meal on the table in less than 30 minutes. Larger beef roasts are perfect for the gourmet weekend cook.

Beef Steaks

Tender beef steaks

Beef (Loin or Rib) steaks are the most tender beef steaks for grilling. Choose **rib-eye, rib, T-bone, porterhouse, top loin (strip), tenderloin** or **top sirloin.**

Economical, less tender steaks

Flank, skirt, top round and **boneless chuck shoulder steaks** have fabulous flavor on the grill. For best results, use a tenderizing marinade and only cook them to medium-rare doneness (145°F).

Beef Roasts

Larger cuts of beef such as **rib-eye roast, whole tenderloin, tri-tip, brisket** and **round tip** are a weekend cook's delight. Most roasts benefit from indirect cooking to achieve a smoky, savory flavor and increased tenderness. Try smoking a brisket or use the rotisserie for rib-eye or sirloin tip roasts. Both **tenderloin** and **tri-tip roasts** can be cooked to perfection over direct heat.

IS IT DONE IF IT'S RED?

Grilled meat and poultry, especially if smoked, can look pink even when well done. Or, there may be a pink-colored rim about ½ inch wide around the outside of the cooked meat. Follow cooking times and temperatures closely when cooking meats. Use a thermometer to check the temperature to determine doneness.

GREAT GRILLED STEAKS

Steaks are the number one favorite of America's backyard cooks. Follow these simple guidelines to help ensure your steaks are grilled to perfection.

1. Trim off all but about ¼ inch of visible fat to prevent flare-ups.

2. Pat steaks dry with paper towels to help them brown quickly.

3. Make sure coals are ash-covered or the gas grill is preheated to brown the meat when you place it on the grid. Reduce heat to medium or medium-high to make sure the inside cooks before the outside gets charred.

4. Use tongs to turn the meat. If you pierce a steak with a fork, it will lose flavorful juices.

5. For best results, cook beef steaks to 145°F for medium-rare or 160°F for medium doneness.

6. Do not overcook steaks. Follow the cooking times suggested in the recipe.

7. The best way to determine doneness of a steak is with an instant-read thermometer inserted horizontally from the side into the center.

8. Let the steaks rest for 2 to 3 minutes before you serve them. This allows the juices to flow back from the center of the meat to the exterior, giving you a moist, juicy steak.

Better Burgers

Whether you're using ground beef, pork, turkey, chicken or lamb, or a special mixture of ground meats, the general techniques are the same.

1. **Form the patties gently but firmly** for tender juicy patties. Overworking patties creates a firm, compact and tough texture.

2. **Make the right size patties.** Form patties ½ inch thick. Food safety requires that the interior of a burger reaches a temperature of at least 160°F. A really thick burger is likely to be burned outside before it reaches that temperature inside.

3. **Make patties ½ inch larger than the buns.** Patties will shrink a little during grilling (losing some fat and water). If you make them larger than the bun, you'll have the perfect fit.

4. **Properly prepare the grill.** Clean and oil the grid. Preheat the grill to medium.

5. **Season just before cooking.** Salt draws moisture out of the patties. Season just before or right after cooking.

6. **Leave the burgers on the grill for 3 or 4 minutes before turning.** Then they will release from the grid and be easier to turn.

7. **Keep in the juices.** Don't press the patties! Flavorful juices will be lost. Turn with a spatula or tongs, not a fork.

8. **Use a thermometer to check the temperature.** Use an instant-read thermometer inserted horizontally into the side of burgers to check doneness. (Remember to remove an instant read thermometer after using it or it will melt on the grill.) The color of the patty interior is not a reliable way to judge food safety. Check the chart below for various cooking times and doneness temperatures.

9. **Remove from the grill to a clean platter.** To avoid cross-contamination with raw meat and juices from the original platter, put the patties on a clean plate or platter.

10. **Serve with fabulous toppings!**

BURGER COOKING TIMES & TEMPERATURES*

Type of Meat	Thickness	Total Grilling Time	Internal End Temperature
Ground Beef Patties	½ inch thick	11 to 13 minutes (charcoal, uncovered) 7 to 8 minutes (gas, covered)	160°F
Ground Poultry (Turkey & Chicken) Patties	½ inch thick	10 to 12 minutes	165°F
Ground Pork Patties	½ inch thick	8 to 10 minutes	160°F
Ground Lamb Patties	½ inch thick	10 minutes	160°F

*USDA (United States Department of Agriculture) safe internal temperatures for meat and poultry.

Pork on the Patio

Pork is so easy to grill and so delectable. Since many pork cuts are lean, do not overcook them. Use marinades to add moisture and seasoning rubs for delicious flavor.

Pork Chops (Loin or Rib) are cut in various forms—thick or thin, bone-in or butterflied. Pork chops cook quickly (under 30 minutes) over direct heat.

Pork Loin and Pork Tenderloin Roasts are great for kabobs but are even better as roasts. Larger pork loin roasts need to be cooked over low indirect heat. Pork tenderloins are small and thin enough to cook over medium-high direct heat.

IT'S STILL PINK. IS IT DONE?

All pork cuts should be grilled to 145°F (medium doneness). Cuts like pork tenderloin can be removed from the grill at 140°F and allowed to stand, covered, until the temperature rises to 145°F. Standing also allows the juices to redistribute throughout the roast before slicing. Grilled and smoked pork can often remain pink even when well done. It's best to rely on a thermometer to determine doneness.

Bone up on Ribs

Ribs are the ultimate barbecue. Pork ribs are the most popular, but also try tasty beef and lamb ribs.

Pork Rib Types

Pork Back Ribs, or "baby" back ribs are smaller in size than spareribs (about 8 to 14 bones per slab).

Pork Spareribs are larger and heavier than back ribs (about 11 to 14 bones per slab). They are the least meaty, but full of flavor.

Beef Rib Types

Beef Back Ribs are about 6 to 8 inches long with tender meat between the bones (6 to 7 ribs per slab).

Beef Short Ribs, Flanken or Korean-Style Ribs are short ribs cut in 3-rib sections across the rib bones, about ½ inch thick.

Lamb Rib Types

Found in specialty butcher shops, lamb ribs come in two sizes.

Lamb Spareribs, or "Denver-style" ribs, are similar to pork spareribs, but smaller.

Lamb Riblets are spareribs cut down the center into shorter pieces.

Rib Preparation

• Trim off extra fat and remove the tough membrane on the back.

• Cook slowly. Ribs require indirect heat for cooking to reach fall-off-the-bone tenderness (about 1½ hours on a grill rack). Some methods precook or braise the ribs on low in the oven and finish them on the grill with a flavorful sauce.

• Brush on sauces containing sugar only during the last 15 minutes of grilling to prevent burning.

• Add smoky flavor to your ribs by soaking wood chips and placing them over the fire.

• To tell when ribs are done, look for a bit of bone protruding from the meat (about ¼ inch) to see if the meat is tender enough to tear apart with your fingers.

Sausage & Lamb

SAUSAGE

Whether you call them bangers, wieners, frankfurters or brats, sausages become a gourmet meal when grilled. They all fall into one of two categories.

Cooked Sausages: Many sausages are packaged ready-to-eat—hot dogs are the best known in this category, which also includes most smoked sausages. If labeled "fully cooked", they just need to be heated through and nicely browned on the grill.

Raw or Fresh Sausages: Old-fashioned bratwurst, Italian sausage and kielbasa (Polish) sausage are often sold uncooked.

These sausages require special handling for food safety reasons. They should be kept separate from cooked food and need to be cooked all the way through (160°F). Sausages may also be poached or braised first in beer or another flavorful liquid, then heated and browned on the grill.

LUXURIOUS LAMB

Because of its natural tenderness, lamb is ideal for grilling.

Lamb Chops (Rib and Loin) are the most popular for grilling. They should be at least 1 inch thick.

Lamb Cubes for Skewers should be from the leg and cut into uniform sizes.

Butterflied Leg of Lamb is the all-time classic grilled roast for grilling aficionados. The leg, completely boned, and excess fat removed, resembles a butterfly when spread flat on the grill. This provides a natural range of "doneness"—the thickest portion being rare, the middle medium, and the thinnest portions well done.

Poultry Perfection

Understanding that white meat cooks faster than dark and different size pieces take different amounts of time is the key to cooking poultry.

Chicken

Boneless Skinless Chicken Breasts cook quickly on the grill. But beware, they will overcook and get tough in a matter of seconds.

Leg Parts are ideal for grilling because they contain more fat than white meat, which helps keep them moist.

Boneless Skinless Thighs can be used in place of boneless breasts in most recipes.

Bone-In Drumsticks, Thighs and Leg Parts are popular cuts that cook more quickly than a whole chicken. Each part cooks differently depending on its size.

Whole or Half Chickens require indirect heat. It will take more than an hour to cook succulent and flavorful chicken.

Turkey

To grill a Whole Turkey, make sure that the bird you buy is small enough to fit comfortably under the lid of your grill with at least one inch to spare. Buy a bird under 16 pounds because it takes bigger birds too long to reach an internal temperature that will destroy harmful bacteria. Whole turkeys require long cooking with medium indirect heat.

Bone-In Turkey Breast cooks much faster than a whole turkey.

Turkey Tenderloins or Cutlets, smaller boneless cuts, cook quickly over direct heat.

Seafood Savvy

Steaks or Fillets?

When buying fish, consider the cut—a steak versus a fillet.

Fish Steak is a crosscut section, often including a piece of the backbone. Steaks are the most forgiving on the grill since they are thick and compact—and less likely to fall apart than a fillet. Many fish aren't available in steak form since they're too small to be cut this way.

Fillets are usually less bony and somewhat easier to eat. If you are grilling fillets, it is helpful to use a fish basket or grill topper.

Choose the Right Variety of Fish

Virtually any fish can be grilled, but some varieties, such as sole or flounder, are so delicate they just aren't a good choice.

Salmon is America's favorite fish. The rich, full flavor is perfect when enhanced with a touch of smoke from the grill.

Tuna: Like salmon, tuna is a fairly fatty fish, so it does well on the grill. It is only available as a steak. Tuna is often served seared on the outside and rare on the inside, because it becomes tough and flavorless if cooked too long. If you prefer your fish cooked through, grill a thinner (½-inch) steak.

Swordfish, a mild, firm-fleshed fish, is usually sold in the form of a steak. It takes well to marinades and is firm enough to skewer for kabobs.

Halibut: Halibut is a firm white fish usually sold as fillets. It's a good grilling fish, but leaner and more delicate than swordfish or salmon.

Snapper and Sea Bass are firm white fish, mild in flavor, sold as fillets or steaks. They can be used interchangeably in most recipes.

Catfish and Trout are usually farm raised, so they're very affordable. The fillets can fall apart fairly easily when you try to turn them, but they are usually thin enough to cook through without flipping.

Shellfish—Shrimp, Lobster and Scallops

Don't overcook shellfish. Shrimp are done when they turn uniformly pink. Lobster and scallops should be cooked only until opaque in the center. Be especially careful with scallops, which cook quickly and become rubbery in a matter of seconds.

Seafood Grilling Guide

Fish cooks best over medium-high heat; shellfish requires high heat.

• Liberally brush oil on the grid and oil fish lightly just before cooking.

• Turn only once and not too soon. The time to turn is when the fish releases naturally from the grid. This generally takes from 5 to 7 minutes.

• Use a grill topper or fish basket to keep flaky fish or smaller shellfish from falling though the grid.

• Cook until just opaque throughout. Fish continues to cook after it's removed from the heat.

┌─────── **DON'T OVERCOOK!** ───────┐

So how do you tell when the fish is done? Peek. Take a knife and gently part the flesh at the thickest part just enough to see inside. The flesh should be just opaque all the way through. (If you grill until the fish "flakes easily" you'll end up with dried-out fish.)

└──────────────────────────────────┘

Vegetables and Fruit

Grilling brings the taste of ordinary fruits and vegetables to luscious new levels. The direct heat concentrates flavors by cooking out water and caramelizing the natural plant sugars.

Grilling Vegetables

Most vegetables cook quickly and easily over direct medium heat (exceptions are root and other large, dense vegetables). Vegetables need a bit of oil to keep them from sticking to the grid and to maximize flavor. Make your work easier by cutting pieces into similar sizes. You can also help even out cooking times by cutting slower cooking vegetables into thinner pieces or parcooking them first in the microwave. Whatever methods you choose, it won't be hard to convince anyone to eat their vegetables when they're hot off the grill.

Fruit Meets Flame

Fruit can be a sweet surprise when it's touched by the fire. Although you can grill many types of fruits, the ones below are the easiest. Turn grilled fruit into a show-stopping dessert—just serve it with some ice cream or drizzle it with honey.

Bananas: Choose fruit that's still a little green at the ends for best results. Cut unpeeled bananas in half lengthwise and leave the skin on to protect the tender fruit while grilling.

Peaches or Nectarines: Cut slightly underripe fruit into halves and grill it over medium heat for about 10 minutes. Grilled peaches go well with vanilla ice cream and also make a tasty addition to a fruit salsa or salad.

Pineapple: If you only grill one fruit, make it pineapple. Grill rings or wedges for a wonderfully tangy taste. To make it even more irresistible, baste with a bit of brown sugar and rum while it cooks. Pineapple rings that are ½ inch thick cook in 10 minutes or less.

Rubs and Marinades

Rubs are pressed onto the surface of meat before grilling to season and help build a flavorful crust on the exterior of meat. Rubs can be applied just before cooking, or for increased flavor, apply the rub and refrigerate several hours before grilling.

• **Dry rubs** are dry seasonings held together with small amounts of wet ingredients such as oil, crushed garlic or another liquid.

Marinades are seasoned liquid mixtures that add flavor and, in some cases, tenderize. Marinades also moisten the surface of the meat and poultry to prevent it from drying out.

• A **flavoring marinade** is used with tender cuts of meat and poultry for a short time, 15 minutes to 2 hours.

• A **tenderizing marinade** is used with less tender cuts of meat and poultry. Tenderizing marinades include an acidic ingredient for tenderizing, such as wine, vinegar or lemon juice, or a tendering enzyme found in fresh ginger, pineapple and kiwi.

How to marinate: The easiest way to marinate is to place the food in a resealable food storage bag. You can also marinate in a glass or other nonreactive dish. Turn the food once or twice to redistribute the marinade.

How long to marinate? When using a flavoring marinade for foods that do not need tenderizing such as fish, vegetables and tender meats, marinate for only short periods of time (15 minutes to 2 hours). For tenderizing meats and poultry, marinate a few hours to overnight.

Caution: Some marinades, especially those with a tenderizing ingredient like ginger, yogurt, buttermilk, citrus juice, wine or tomato sauce, can result in a mushy texture. Do not marinate with these ingredients for more than 24 hours.

MARINATE SAFELY

• Always marinate all meats in the refrigerator.
• If a marinade will be used later for basting or served as a sauce, reserve some of the marinade before adding it to the meat.
• Never save or reuse a marinade.

• A marinade that has been in contact with uncooked meat must be brought to a full rolling boil and boiled for at least 1 minute before it can be used as a sauce or baste.

Backyard
Beef

Carne Asada

2 boneless beef top loin (strip) steaks, cut 1 inch thick (about 10 ounces each)
2 teaspoons ground cumin
2 large cloves garlic, minced
2 lime wedges
½ to 1 cup prepared guacamole
   Additional lime wedges (optional)

1. Combine cumin and garlic; press evenly onto beef steaks.

2. Place steaks on grid over medium, ash-covered coals. Grill, uncovered, 15 to 18 minutes for medium rare to medium doneness, turning occasionally.

3. Squeeze juice from 1 lime wedge over each steak. Carve steaks into thin slices. Serve with guacamole; garnish with lime wedges, if desired.   *Makes 4 servings*

Tip: To broil, place steaks on rack in broiler pan so surface of beef is 3 to 4 inches from heat. Broil 13 to 17 minutes for medium rare to medium doneness, turning once.

Prep and Cook Time: 20 to 25 minutes

Favorite recipe from **National Cattlemen's Beef Association on behalf of The Beef Checkoff**

East Meets West Burgers

  1 pound ground beef (95% lean)
¼ cup soft whole wheat bread crumbs
  1 large egg white
¼ teaspoon salt
⅛ teaspoon black pepper
  4 whole wheat hamburger buns, split

SESAME-SOY MAYONNAISE:
  ¼ cup light mayonnaise
  1 tablespoon thinly sliced green onion, green part only
  ½ teaspoon soy sauce
  ¼ teaspoon dark sesame oil
  ⅛ teaspoon ground red pepper

SLAW TOPPING:
  ½ cup romaine lettuce, thinly sliced
  ¼ cup shredded red cabbage
  ¼ cup shredded carrot
  1 teaspoon rice vinegar
  1 teaspoon vegetable oil
  ¼ teaspoon black pepper

1. Combine Sesame-Soy Mayonnaise ingredients in small bowl; refrigerate until ready to use. Combine Slaw Topping ingredients in small bowl; set aside.

2. Combine ground beef, bread crumbs, egg white, salt and ⅛ teaspoon black pepper in large bowl, mixing lightly but thoroughly. Lightly shape into four ½-inch-thick patties.

3. Place patties on grid over medium, ash-covered coals. Grill, uncovered, 11 to 13 minutes to medium (160°F) doneness, until no longer pink in center and juices show no pink color, turning occasionally. About 2 minutes before burgers are done, place buns, cut sides down, on grid. Grill until lightly toasted.

4. Spread equal amount of mayonnaise on bottom of each bun; top with burger. Evenly divide Slaw Topping over burgers. Close sandwiches.

Makes 4 servings

Tip: To make soft bread crumbs, place torn bread in food processor or blender container. Cover; process, pulsing on and off, to form fine crumbs. One and one-half slices makes about 1 cup crumbs.

Prep and Cook Time: 30 to 40 minutes

Favorite recipe from **National Cattlemen's Beef Association on behalf of The Beef Checkoff**

Tuscan Beef

1 tablespoon olive oil
2 cloves garlic, minced
1½ teaspoons dried rosemary, divided
1 teaspoon salt
½ teaspoon black pepper
4 boneless beef rib-eye or top loin (strip) steaks (8 to 10 ounces each), cut ¾ to 1 inch thick
¾ cup tomato-basil or marinara pasta sauce
½ cup sliced pimiento-stuffed green olives
1 tablespoon drained capers

1. Prepare grill for direct cooking. Combine oil, garlic, 1 teaspoon rosemary, salt and pepper in small bowl; mix well. Spread mixture evenly over both sides of steaks.

2. Grill steaks, covered, over medium-high heat 8 to 10 minutes for medium-rare (145°F) or to desired doneness, turning once.

3. Meanwhile, combine pasta sauce, olives, capers and remaining ½ teaspoon rosemary in small saucepan. Heat over medium-low heat until hot but not boiling. Transfer steaks to serving plates; top with sauce.

Makes 4 servings

Note: The sodium content of prepared pasta sauces varies widely. Since olives and capers also add salty flavors to this recipe, choose a product with lower sodium for best results.

 TOOL TIP The most accurate way to determine doneness of steaks and chops is with an instant-read thermometer. Hold the steak with tongs and insert the thermometer horizontally from the side into the center. Cover the indentation on the stem to ensure the thermometer will accurately measure the temperature. And be sure to remove the thermometer from the steak if additional cooking is required. It will melt if left in the steak.

Texas Smoked BBQ Brisket

½ cup prepared barbecue seasoning
2 tablespoons ground chili powder
1 (5- to 7-pound) beef brisket, trimmed with a layer of fat (center flat portion)
1 cup *Frank's® RedHot® Chile 'n Lime™* Hot Sauce or *Frank's® RedHot®* Cayenne
    Pepper Sauce
1½ cups beer or non-alcoholic malt beverage, divided
1 cup *Cattlemen's®* Authentic Smoke House Barbecue Sauce or *Cattlemen's®* Award
    Winning Classic Barbecue Sauce
¼ cup butter

1. Combine barbecue seasoning and chili powder. Rub mixture thoroughly into beef. Place meat, fat-side up, into disposable foil pan. Cover and refrigerate 1 to 3 hours. Just before using, prepare mop sauce by combining *Chile 'n Lime™* Hot Sauce and 1 cup beer; set aside.

2. Prepare grill for indirect cooking over medium-low heat (250°F). If desired, toss soaked wood chips over coals or heat source. Place pan with meat in center of grill over indirect heat. Cover grill. Cook meat, over low heat 6 to 7 hours until meat is very tender (190°F internal temperature). Baste with mop sauce once an hour.

3. Combine barbecue sauce, butter and remaining ½ cup beer. Simmer 5 minutes until slightly thickened. Slice meat and serve with sauce.
    Makes 10 to 12 servings

Tip: To easily slice meat, cut against the grain using an electric knife.

Prep Time: 15 minutes • **Marinate Time:** 1 hour • **Cook Time:** 7 hours

 TIP Grilled meat and poultry, especially smoked, can look pink even when well done. Or there may be a pink-colored rim about one-half inch wide around the outside of the cooked meat. Follow cooking times and temperatures closely when cooking meats. Use a thermometer to check the internal temperature to determine doneness.

Cuban-Style Marinated Skirt Steak

    2 pounds skirt steaks, cut into 6-inch pieces
    2 cups orange juice, divided
    ½ cup lemon juice
    ½ cup lime juice
    ¼ cup olive oil
    5 cloves garlic, minced
    1 teaspoon dried oregano
    2 teaspoons grated orange peel, plus additional for garnish
    1 large onion, cut into thin wedges
    3 cups cooked white rice
    3 cups cooked black beans

1. Place steaks in large resealable food storage bag. Mix 1 cup orange juice, lemon juice, lime juice, oil, garlic and oregano in medium bowl; reserve ½ cup. Pour remaining juice mixture over steaks. Seal bag; turn to coat. Marinate in refrigerator 30 to 60 minutes.

2. Mix remaining 1 cup orange juice and 2 teaspoons orange peel in separate medium bowl. Add onion; marinate 30 minutes.

3. Prepare grill for direct cooking. Remove steaks; discard marinade. Grill steaks, covered, over medium heat 8 to 12 minutes or to desired doneness, turning once. Remove to cutting board. Tent with foil; let stand 5 minutes before slicing.

4. Slice each steak against the grain into thin slices. Transfer slices to serving platter. Remove onions from orange juice; arrange on top of meat. Sprinkle with reserved juice mixture and additional orange peel. Serve with rice and black beans.

Makes 6 servings

 TIP Traditionally used for fajitas, skirt steaks are long, narrow, thin cuts of meat with a distinct visible grain. They are easier to grill if cut into smaller portions. For maximum tenderness, cut cooked steaks against the grain into thin slices. Tilt the knife diagonally when cutting to ensure the largest surface area possible for each slice.

Cavemen Beef Back Ribs

¼ cup paprika
¼ cup brown sugar
¼ cup seasoned salt
2 full racks beef back ribs, split in half (about 6 to 8 pounds)
1 cup *Cattlemen's*® Authentic Smoke House Barbecue Sauce
¼ cup apple, pineapple or orange juice

1. Combine paprika, sugar and seasoned salt. Rub mixture into ribs. Cover ribs and refrigerate 1 to 3 hours.

2. Prepare grill for indirect cooking over medium-low heat (250°F). Place ribs on rib rack or in foil pan. Cook on covered grill 2½ to 3 hours until very tender.

3. Meanwhile, combine barbecue sauce and juice. Brush mixture on ribs during last 30 minutes of cooking. Serve with additional barbecue sauce.   *Makes 6 to 8 servings*

Tip: For very tender ribs, remove membrane from underside of ribs before cooking. With a sharp paring knife, score membrane on bone from underside of ribs. Lift up portions of membrane with point of knife. Using kitchen towel, pull membrane away from bone and discard.

Prep Time: 5 minutes • Marinate Time: 1 hour • Cook Time: 3 hours

Cheesy Spinach Burgers

1 envelope LIPTON® RECIPE SECRETS® Onion Soup Mix
2 pounds ground beef
1 package (10 ounces) frozen chopped spinach, thawed and squeezed dry
1 cup shredded mozzarella or Cheddar cheese (about 4 ounces)

1. In large bowl, combine all ingredients; shape into 8 patties.

2. Grill or broil until no longer pink in center (160°F). Serve, if desired, on hamburger buns.
Makes 8 servings

Cavemen Beef Back Ribs

Grilled Steak with Mango Salsa

1 pound beef top round steak, cut ¾ inch thick
4 cups hot cooked couscous
2 cups sugar snap peas, steamed

MARINADE:
¼ cup fresh lime juice
2 tablespoons minced green onion
2 tablespoons water
1 tablespoon vegetable oil
2 teaspoons minced fresh ginger
2 cloves garlic, minced
¼ teaspoon salt

MANGO SALSA:
1½ cups finely diced fresh mango
2 tablespoons minced green onion
1 tablespoon fresh lime juice
1 tablespoon minced fresh cilantro
1 red serrano or red jalapeño pepper, seeded, finely chopped

1. Combine marinade ingredients. Place beef steak and marinade in food-safe plastic bag; turn steak to coat. Close bag securely and marinate in refrigerator 6 hours or as long as overnight, turning occasionally.

2. Just before grilling steak, combine salsa ingredients in medium bowl. Cover and refrigerate until ready to serve.

3. Remove steak from marinade; discard marinade. Place steak on grid over medium, ash-covered coals. Grill, covered, about 8 to 9 minutes for medium rare doneness, turning occasionally.

4. Carve steak into thin slices. Season with salt and pepper, as desired. Serve with salsa, couscous and sugar snap peas.

Makes 4 servings

Prep and Cook Time: 1 hour • **Marinate Time:** 6 hours or overnight

Favorite recipe from **National Cattlemen's Beef Association on behalf of The Beef Checkoff**

Backyard Barbecue Burgers

1½ pounds ground beef
⅓ cup barbecue sauce, divided
1 onion, sliced
1 tomato, sliced
2 tablespoons olive oil
6 kaiser rolls, split
6 leaves green or red leaf lettuce

1. Prepare grill for direct cooking. Combine ground beef and 2 tablespoons barbecue sauce in large bowl. Shape into six 1-inch-thick patties.

2. Grill patties, covered, over medium heat 8 to 10 minutes (or uncovered 13 to 15 minutes) for medium doneness (160°F), turning occasionally. Brush both sides with remaining barbecue sauce during last 5 minutes of cooking.

3. Meanwhile, brush onion* and tomato slices with oil. Place on grid. Grill onion slices about 10 minutes and tomato slices 2 to 3 minutes.

4. Just before serving, place rolls, cut side down, on grid; grill until lightly toasted. Serve patties on rolls with tomatoes, onions and lettuce. *Makes 6 servings*

*Onion slices may be cooked on the stove. Heat 2 tablespoons oil in a large skillet over medium heat; add onions and cook 10 minutes or until tender and slightly brown, stirring frequently.

Grilled Steak with Creamy Herbed Chavrie® Topping

1 package (5 ounces) CHAVRIE® goat cheese, plain
1 tablespoon chopped fresh chives
1 tablespoon chopped fresh parsley
1 tablespoon fresh basil chiffonade*
4 beef tenderloin, T-bone or sirloin steaks
1 garlic clove, crushed
Salt and pepper

*To make a chiffonade, stack basil leaves and roll up like a jelly roll. Cut into thin slices.

In small bowl, mix *Chavrie®*, chives, parsley and basil. Rub all surfaces of steaks with garlic and season to taste with salt and pepper. Grill over medium-high heat or broil 4 to 6 inches from heat to desired doneness. Spoon herbed Chavrie® over steaks. *Makes 4 servings*

Backyard Barbecue Burgers

Espresso-Bourbon Steaks with Mashed Sweet Potatoes

4 beef tenderloin steaks, cut 1 inch thick (about 4 ounces each)
2 to 4 teaspoons coarsely cracked black pepper
   Mashed Sweet Potatoes (recipe follows)
   Steamed green beans

ESPRESSO-BOURBON SAUCE:
   ¼ cup bourbon
   ¼ cup maple syrup
   ¼ cup reduced sodium soy sauce
   1 tablespoon fresh lemon juice
   2 teaspoons instant espresso coffee powder
   ⅛ teaspoon black pepper

1. Combine all sauce ingredients, except pepper, in small saucepan; bring to a boil. Reduce heat and simmer, uncovered, 12 to 15 minutes or until sauce is thickened and reduced by about half, stirring occasionally. Stir in pepper. Keep warm.

2. Prepare Mashed Sweet Potatoes. Meanwhile, press coarsely cracked pepper on both sides of beef steak. Place steaks on grid over medium, ash-covered coals. Grill, uncovered, 13 to 15 minutes for medium rare doneness, turning once.

3. Evenly divide sauce among 4 plates. Place steak on top of sauce. Serve with Mashed Sweet Potatoes and green beans. *Makes 4 servings*

Mashed Sweet Potatoes: Place 9 ounces peeled and cubed sweet potatoes and 1 teaspoon salt in large saucepan. Cover with water; bring to a boil. Cook 4 to 5 minutes or until potatoes are tender. Drain. Combine potatoes, 2 tablespoons butter, ⅛ teaspoon salt and ⅛ teaspoon black pepper. Beat until mashed and smooth.

Tip: To broil, place steaks on rack in broiler pan so surface of beef is 2 to 3 inches from heat. Broil 13 to 16 minutes for medium rare to medium doneness, turning once.

Prep and Cook Time: 45 minutes

Favorite recipe from **National Cattlemen's Beef Association on behalf of The Beef Checkoff**

Grilled Steak with Arugula & Gorgonzola Salad

    4 beef top loin (strip) steaks (¾ inch thick)
    1 cup balsamic or red wine salad dressing, divided
  16 large arugula leaves *or* 1½ cups baby arugula leaves
  1½ cups mixed salad greens
    ⅓ cup crumbled Gorgonzola cheese

1. Place steaks in large resealable food storage bag; pour ½ cup salad dressing into bag. Seal bag; turn to coat. Marinate in refrigerator 20 to 30 minutes.

2. Prepare grill for direct cooking. Remove steaks; discard marinade. Grill steaks, covered, over medium heat 7 to 12 minutes for medium-rare (145°F) or to desired doneness, turning once.

3. Meanwhile, combine arugula and salad greens in large bowl. Pour remaining ½ cup dressing over greens; toss until greens are well coated. Serve steaks with salad. Sprinkle cheese over salad and steaks.

Makes 4 servings

Greek-Style Steak Sandwiches

    2 teaspoons Greek seasoning or dried oregano
    1 beef flank steak (about 1½ pounds)
    4 pita bread rounds, sliced in half crosswise
    1 small cucumber, thinly sliced
  ½ cup sliced red onion
  ½ cup chopped tomato
  ½ cup crumbled feta cheese
  ¼ cup red wine vinaigrette
    1 cup plain yogurt

1. Rub Greek seasoning all over steak. Place on plate; cover and refrigerate 30 to 60 minutes.

2. Prepare grill for direct cooking. Grill steaks, covered, over medium heat 15 to 20 minutes or to desired doneness, turning once. Transfer to cutting board. Tent with foil; let stand 10 minutes before slicing.

3. Meanwhile, grill pitas 1 minute per side or until warm. Slice steak against the grain into thin strips; divide meat among pitas. Top each with cucumber, onion, tomato and feta cheese; drizzle with vinaigrette and top with yogurt.

Makes 8 sandwiches

Grilled Steak with Arugula & Gorgonzola Salad

Blue Cheese & Bacon Stuffed Cheeseburgers

     4 slices applewood smoked bacon
     1 small red onion, finely chopped
     2 tablespoons crumbled blue cheese
     1 tablespoon butter, softened
  1½ pounds ground beef
       Salt and black pepper
     4 onion or regular hamburger rolls
       Lettuce leaves

1. Cook bacon in large skillet over medium-high heat until almost crisp. Remove to paper towels to drain; finely chop bacon. Place in small bowl. Add onion to skillet; cook and stir about 5 minutes or until soft. Add to bowl with bacon; cool slightly. Stir in blue cheese and butter until well blended.

2. Prepare grill for direct cooking.

3. Divide ground beef into eight equal portions. Flatten into thin patties about 4 inches wide; season with salt and pepper. Place 2 tablespoons bacon mixture in center of one patty; cover with another patty. Pinch edges together to seal. Shape burger until round and slightly flattened. Repeat with remaining patties and bacon mixture.

4. Grill patties, covered, over medium heat 8 to 10 minutes (or uncovered 13 to 15 minutes) for medium doneness (160°F), turning once. Transfer to platter; let stand 2 minutes before serving. Serve burgers on rolls with lettuce.   *Makes 4 servings*

TIP If you want juicy flavorful burgers, do not flatten the patties. Pressing down on the patties with a spatula not only squeezes out tasty juices, but for this recipe the stuffing might pop out.

Classic Fajitas

1 beef flank or skirt steak (1½ pounds)
2 large onions, cut into ½-inch slices
2 medium green bell peppers, cut into quarters
12 small flour tortillas (6- to 7-inch diameter), warmed
   Salt and pepper
   Prepared guacamole (optional)

MARINADE:
1 package (about 1.25 ounces) fajita seasoning mix
¼ cup water
2 tablespoons fresh lime juice

1. Combine marinade ingredients in small bowl. Place beef steak and marinade in food-safe plastic bag; turn steak to coat. Close bag securely and marinate in refrigerator 6 hours or as long as overnight, turning occasionally.

2. Remove steak from marinade; discard marinade. Place steak in center of grid over medium, ash-covered coals; arrange onions and bell peppers around steak. Grill flank steak, uncovered, 17 to 21 minutes (skirt steak 10 to 13 minutes) for medium rare to medium doneness, turning occasionally. Grill vegetables 13 to 16 minutes or until crisp-tender, turning occasionally.

3. Carve flank steak lengthwise in half, then crosswise into thin slices. (Carve skirt steak diagonally across the grain into thin slices.) Cut bell peppers into ½-inch strips; coarsely chop onions. Place steak slices on tortillas; top with vegetables. Season with salt and pepper, as desired. Serve with guacamole, if desired.

Makes 6 servings

Tip: Wrap tortillas in heavy-duty foil and place on grid over medium, ash-covered coals. Grill 5 minutes or until warm, turning occasionally. Keep warm until ready to serve.

Prep and Cook Time: 40 to 45 minutes • Marinate Time: 6 hours or overnight

Favorite recipe from **National Cattlemen's Beef Association on behalf of The Beef Checkoff**

Cucumber Ranch Steaks

4 beef shoulder center steaks (Ranch Steak), cut ¾ inch thick (about 5 ounces each)
½ cup finely chopped seeded cucumber
¼ cup prepared ranch dressing
1 tablespoon garlic-pepper seasoning
1 small tomato, seeded, diced (optional)

1. Combine cucumber and dressing in small bowl. Set aside.

2. Press garlic-pepper seasoning evenly onto beef steaks. Place steaks on grid over medium, ash-covered coals. Grill, covered, 9 to 11 minutes for medium rare to medium doneness, turning once.

3. Serve steaks with cucumber sauce. Garnish with tomato.   *Makes 4 servings*

Tip: To easily seed a cucumber, cut it lengthwise in half and use the tip of a teaspoon to scrape out the seeds. European or English greenhouse-grown cucumbers, available in many supermarkets, are virtually seedless.

Prep and Cook Time: 25 to 30 minutes

Favorite recipe from **National Cattlemen's Beef Association on behalf of The Beef Checkoff**

Grilled Mexican Steak

¾ cup Italian salad dressing
½ cup *Frank's® RedHot® Chile 'n Lime*™ Hot Sauce
½ cup fresh cilantro or parsley, minced
1 teaspoon dried oregano leaves
2 cloves garlic, minced
2 pound boneless sirloin, 1½ inches thick
   Flour tortillas, heated

1. Place salad dressing, *Chile 'n Lime*™ Hot Sauce, cilantro, oregano and garlic in blender or food processor. Cover and process until well blended. Reserve ¾ cup of the sauce mixture. Place steak in large resealable plastic food storage bag. Pour remaining sauce mixture over steak. Seal bag and marinate in refrigerator 30 minutes.

2. Place steak on rack, discarding marinade. Grill over high heat 10 minutes per side for medium-rare or to desired doneness. Let steak stand 5 minutes. Slice steak diagonally. Serve with reserved sauce mixture and warm tortillas.   *Makes 6 to 8 servings*

Prep Time: 10 minutes • Marinate Time: 30 minutes • Cook Time: 20 minutes

Cucumber Ranch Steaks

Caesar Salad Beef Burgers on Garlic Crostini

1½ pounds ground beef
3 cloves garlic, minced
1 teaspoon salt
½ teaspoon pepper
4 Romaine lettuce leaves
¼ cup freshly shaved or grated Parmesan cheese

GARLIC CROSTINI:
8 slices sourdough bread (about 4×3×½-inch)
Extra-virgin olive oil
2 large cloves garlic, cut lengthwise into quarters

1. Combine ground beef, minced garlic, 1 teaspoon salt and ½ teaspoon pepper in large bowl, mixing lightly but thoroughly. Lightly shape into four ¾-inch thick patties, shaping to fit the bread slices.

2. Place patties on grid over medium, ash-covered coals. Grill, uncovered, 13 to 15 minutes to medium (160°F) doneness, until not pink in center and juices show no pink color, turning occasionally. Season with salt and pepper, as desired.

3. Meanwhile, brush both sides of bread slices lightly with oil. Place bread around outer edge of grid. Grill a few minutes until lightly toasted, turning once. Remove bread slices from grid; rub both sides of each slice with a garlic quarter.

4. Place one lettuce leaf on four of the bread slices; top each with a burger. Sprinkle evenly with cheese; cover with remaining bread slices. Cut burgers in half; arrange on lettuce-lined platter, if desired.

Makes 4 servings

Tip: Use a vegetable peeler to quickly shave Parmesan cheese.

Prep and Cook Time: 30 minutes

Favorite recipe from **National Cattlemen's Beef Association on behalf of The Beef Checkoff**

Drunken T-Bone Steak

  2 T-bone steaks, cut 1-inch thick (about 3 pounds)
  1 cup *French's®* Worcestershire Sauce
  ½ cup *Cattlemen's®* Authentic Smoke House Barbecue Sauce
  3 tablespoons bourbon
  2 tablespoons butter
  2 tablespoons *French's®* Worcestershire Sauce
  4 teaspoons garlic and pepper steak seasoning

1. Place steaks into resealable plastic food storage bag. Pour 1 cup Worcestershire over steaks. Marinate in refrigerator 1 to 3 hours.

2. Meanwhile, prepare sauce. Combine barbecue sauce, bourbon, butter and 2 tablespoons Worcestershire in saucepan. Heat to boiling. Simmer 3 minutes; reserve.

3. Drain steaks. Rub steak seasoning into meat, coating both sides. Cook steaks over high direct heat, about 7 minutes per side for medium-rare (145°F) or to desired doneness. Let steaks rest 10 minutes before slicing. Serve with sauce on the side. *Makes 4 servings*

Prep Time: 5 minutes • Cook Time: 15 minutes • Marinate Time: 1 hour

Peppercorn Steaks

  2 tablespoons olive oil
  1 to 2 teaspoons cracked pink or black peppercorns or ground black pepper
  1 teaspoon dried herbs, such as rosemary or parsley
  1 teaspoon minced garlic
  4 boneless beef top loin (strip) or rib eye steaks
  ¼ teaspoon salt

1. Combine oil, peppercorns, herbs and garlic in small bowl. Rub mixture all over steaks. Place on plate; cover and refrigerate 30 to 60 minutes.

2. Prepare grill for direct cooking.

3. Grill steaks, uncovered, over medium heat 10 to 12 minutes for medium-rare to medium or to desired doneness, turning once. Season with salt. *Makes 4 servings*

Drunken T-Bone Steak

Sesame-Garlic Flank Steak

  1 beef flank steak (about 1¼ pounds)
¼ cup soy sauce
¼ cup hoisin sauce
  2 tablespoons dark sesame oil
  4 cloves garlic, minced

1. Score steak on both sides lightly with sharp knife in diamond pattern; place in large resealable food storage bag. Combine remaining ingredients in small bowl; pour over steak. Seal bag; turn to coat. Marinate in refrigerator at least 2 hours or up to 24 hours, turning once.

2. Prepare grill for direct cooking. Remove steak from marinade; reserve marinade. Grill steak, covered, over medium heat 13 to 18 minutes for medium-rare to medium or to desired doneness, turning and brushing with marinade halfway through cooking time. Discard remaining marinade.

3. Transfer steak to cutting board; carve against the grain into thin slices. *Makes 4 servings*

Steak au Poivre with Dijon Sauce

  4 beef tenderloin steaks, cut 1½ inches thick (about 1½ pounds)
  1 tablespoon *French's*® Worcestershire Sauce
    Crushed black peppercorns
⅓ cup *French's*® Honey Dijon Mustard
⅓ cup mayonnaise
  3 tablespoons dry red wine
  2 tablespoons finely chopped red or green onion
  2 tablespoons minced fresh parsley
  1 clove garlic, minced

1. Brush steaks with Worcestershire and sprinkle with pepper to taste; set aside. To prepare Dijon Sauce, combine mustard, mayonnaise, wine, onion, parsley and garlic; mix well.

2. Place steaks on grid. Grill over hot coals 15 minutes for medium-rare or to desired doneness, turning often. Serve with Dijon Sauce. *Makes 4 servings*

Note: Dijon Sauce is also great with grilled salmon and swordfish. To serve with fish, substitute white wine for the red wine and minced fresh dill for the parsley.

Prep Time: 10 minutes • Cook Time: 15 minutes

Sesame-Garlic Flank Steak

Dinner on a Stick

 1/4 cup Italian salad dressing
  2 tablespoons Worcestershire sauce
 24 medium whole mushrooms (about 12 ounces)
 12 ounces boneless beef top sirloin steak, cut into 24 (1-inch) cubes
  1 medium zucchini, quartered lengthwise and cut into 24 (1-inch) pieces
  1 medium green bell pepper, cut into 24 (1-inch) pieces

SAUCE
 1/4 cup mayonnaise
 1/4 cup sour cream
  1 clove garlic, minced
 1/4 to 1/2 teaspoon dried rosemary
 1/4 teaspoon salt

1. Combine salad dressing and Worcestershire in small bowl. Reserve 2 tablespoons dressing mixture. Combine mushrooms, beef and remaining dressing mixture in large resealable food storage bag. Seal bag; turn to coat. Marinate in refrigerator 30 to 60 minutes.

2. For sauce, combine mayonnaise, sour cream, garlic, rosemary and salt in small bowl. Cover; refrigerate until ready to serve.

3. Prepare grill for direct cooking. Thread beef, mushrooms, squash and bell pepper alternately onto eight 10-inch skewers; discard remaining marinade.

4. Grill skewers over medium-high heat 6 to 8 minutes or to desired doneness, turning occasionally. Do not overcook.

5. Transfer skewers to serving platter; brush with reserved 2 tablespoons salad dressing mixture. Serve with sauce.

Makes 4 servings

Gazpacho Steak Salad

1 pound beef shoulder steak or 1 pound beef top round steak, cut 1 inch thick
1 can (5½ ounces) spicy 100% vegetable juice
8 cups mixed greens *or* 1 package (10 ounces) romaine and leaf lettuce mixture
1 cup baby pear tomatoes, halved
1 cup cucumber, cut in half lengthwise, then into thin slices
1 cup chopped green bell pepper
   Salt and pepper
   Crunchy Tortilla Strips (recipe follows)

GAZPACHO DRESSING:
   1 can (5½ ounces) spicy 100% vegetable juice
   ½ cup chopped tomato
   ¼ cup finely chopped green bell pepper
   1 tablespoon red wine vinegar
   1 tablespoon chopped cilantro
   2 teaspoons olive oil
   1 clove garlic, minced

1. Place beef steak and 1 can vegetable juice in food-safe plastic bag; turn steak to coat. Close bag securely and marinate in refrigerator 6 hours or as long as overnight.

2. Combine dressing ingredients; refrigerate. Combine greens, baby pear tomatoes, cucumber and 1 cup green bell pepper; refrigerate.

3. Remove steak from marinade; discard marinade. Place steak on grid over medium, ash-covered coals. Grill shoulder steaks, uncovered, 16 to 20 minutes for medium rare to medium doneness (top round steak 16 to 18 minutes for medium rare doneness; do not overcook), turning occasionally. Carve steak across the grain into thin slices. Season with salt and pepper, as desired.

4. Meanwhile prepare Crunchy Tortilla Strips. Add steak to salad mixture. Drizzle with dressing and top with tortilla strips.   *Makes 4 servings*

Crunchy Tortilla Strips: Heat oven to 400°F. Cut 2 corn tortillas in half, then crosswise into ¼-inch wide strips. Place strips in single layer on baking sheet. Bake 4 to 8 minutes or until crisp.

Prep and Cook Time: 30 minutes • Marinate Time: 6 hours or overnight

Favorite recipe from **National Cattlemen's Beef Association on behalf of The Beef Checkoff**

Chipotle-Marinated Beef Flank Steak

1 beef flank steak (about 1½ to 2 pounds) or beef top round steak, cut 1 inch thick (about 1¾ pounds)
Salt

MARINADE:
⅓ cup fresh lime juice
¼ cup chopped fresh cilantro
1 tablespoon packed brown sugar
2 teaspoons minced chipotle chilies in adobo sauce
2 tablespoons adobo sauce (from chilies)
2 cloves garlic, minced
1 teaspoon freshly grated lime peel

1. Combine marinade ingredients in small bowl; mix well. Place beef steak and marinade in food-safe plastic bag; turn steak to coat. Close bag securely and marinate in refrigerator 6 hours or as long as overnight.

2. Remove steak from marinade; discard marinade. Place steak on grid over medium, ash-covered coals. Grill flank steak, uncovered, 17 to 21 minutes for medium rare to medium doneness (top round steak 16 to 18 minutes for medium rare doneness; do not overcook), turning occasionally. Carve steak across the grain into thin slices. Season with salt, as desired.

Makes 4 to 6 servings

Tip: To broil, place steak on rack in broiler pan so surface of beef is 2 to 3 inches from heat. Broil flank steak 13 to 18 minutes for medium rare to medium doneness (top round steak 17 to 18 minutes for medium rare doneness; do not overcook), turning once.

Prep and Cook Time: 30 minutes • Marinate Time: 6 hours or overnight

Favorite recipe from **National Cattlemen's Beef Association on behalf of The Beef Checkoff**

Szechuan Grilled Flank Steak

1 beef flank steak (1¼ to 1½ pounds)
¼ cup seasoned rice wine vinegar
¼ cup soy sauce
2 tablespoons dark sesame oil
4 cloves garlic, minced
2 teaspoons minced fresh ginger
½ teaspoon red pepper flakes
¼ cup water
½ cup thinly sliced green onions
2 to 3 teaspoons sesame seeds, toasted
Hot cooked rice (optional)

1. Place steak in large resealable food storage bag. Combine vinegar, soy sauce, oil, garlic, ginger and red pepper flakes in small bowl; pour over steak. Seal bag; turn to coat. Marinate in refrigerator 3 hours, turning once.

2. Prepare grill for direct cooking. Remove steak from marinade; reserve marinade. Grill steaks, covered, over medium heat 15 to 20 minutes for medium-rare to medium or to desired doneness, turning once.

3. Meanwhile, bring reserved marinade and water to a boil in small saucepan over high heat. Reduce heat to low; simmer 5 minutes. Transfer steak to carving board. Slice against the grain into thin slices. Drizzle slices with boiled marinade. Sprinkle with green onions and sesame seeds. Serve with rice, if desired.   *Makes 4 to 6 servings*

 TIP A heavy resealable food storage bag is ideal for marinating since you can turn the bag instead of each piece of food. In general, the longer you marinate a food the stronger it will taste. Always marinate in the refrigerator.

Korean Beef Short Ribs

2½ pounds beef chuck flanken-style short ribs, cut ⅜ to ½ inch thick*
¼ cup chopped green onions
¼ cup water
¼ cup soy sauce
1 tablespoon sugar
2 teaspoons grated fresh ginger
2 teaspoons dark sesame oil
2 cloves garlic, minced
½ teaspoon black pepper
1 tablespoon sesame seeds, toasted

*Flanken-style ribs can be ordered from your butcher. They are cross-cut short ribs sawed through the bones.

1. Place ribs in large resealable food storage bag. Combine onions, water, soy sauce, sugar, ginger, oil, garlic and pepper in small bowl; pour over ribs. Seal bag; turn to coat. Marinate in refrigerator at least 4 or up to 8 hours, turning occasionally.

2. Prepare grill for direct cooking. Remove ribs; reserve marinade. Grill ribs, covered, over medium-high heat 5 minutes. Brush lightly with reserved marinade; turn and brush again. Discard remaining marinade. Continue to grill, covered, 5 to 6 minutes for medium or to desired doneness. Sprinkle with sesame seeds. *Makes 4 to 6 servings*

Sizzlin' Burgers

1 pound ground beef
¼ cup *French's*® Worcestershire Sauce
½ teaspoon garlic salt
4 hamburger rolls

1. Combine ground beef, Worcestershire and garlic salt; shape into 4 burgers.

2. Grill over medium heat for 15 minutes or until no longer pink in center, turning once.

3. Serve burgers on rolls. Splash on more Worcestershire to taste. *Makes 4 servings*

Korean Beef Short Ribs

Beef Spiedini with Orzo

1½ pounds beef top sirloin steak, cut into 1×1¼-inch pieces
¼ cup olive oil
¼ cup dry red wine
2 cloves garlic, minced
1 teaspoon dried rosemary
1 teaspoon salt, divided
½ teaspoon dried thyme
½ teaspoon coarsely ground black pepper
6 cups water
1 cup uncooked orzo
1 tablespoon butter
1 tablespoon chopped parsley

1. Place beef in large resealable food storage bag. Combine oil, wine, garlic, rosemary, ½ teaspoon salt, thyme and pepper in small bowl; pour over beef. Seal bag; turn to coat. Marinate in refrigerator 15 to 30 minutes.

2. Prepare grill for direct cooking. Soak eight 6- to 8-inch wooden skewers in water 30 minutes.

3. Combine 6 cups water and remaining ½ teaspoon salt in small saucepan; bring to a boil over high heat. Add orzo; reduce heat and simmer 15 minutes or until tender. Drain. Stir in butter and parsley; keep warm.

4. Remove beef from marinade; discard marinade. Thread beef onto skewers. Grill skewers over medium-high heat 8 to 10 minutes, turning occasionally. Serve with orzo.   *Makes 4 servings*

TIP Rosemary skewers and brushes infuse the wonderful scent of rosemary into grilled foods. To make rosemary skewers, find large heavy sprigs and remove the leaves from the bottom three-fourths of the sprigs. Then thread small pieces of meat on each sprig before grilling. Or, to make an aromatic brush, bundle sprigs of rosemary together. Tie with kitchen string and use as a brush for spreading sauces.

Beefy Steak House Salad

1½ cups WISH-BONE® Italian Dressing
2 tablespoons fresh lemon juice
4 tablespoons grated Parmesan cheese
5 cloves garlic, finely chopped
1 tablespoon Worcestershire sauce
1 boneless beef top sirloin steak, 1 inch thick (about 1 pound)
1 large red bell pepper, cut into 1-inch pieces
1 small loaf Italian bread, (about 10 ounces)
10 cups torn romaine lettuce leaves

1. For marinade, blend 1 cup Wish-Bone Italian Dressing, lemon juice, 2 tablespoons cheese, 4 cloves garlic and Worcestershire sauce; set aside. Cut steak into 1¼-inch pieces. In medium, shallow nonaluminum baking dish or plastic bag, pour ⅓ cup marinade over steak and red pepper; turn to coat. Cover, or close bag, and marinate in refrigerator 30 minutes. Reserve remaining marinade.

2. Meanwhile, cut bread lengthwise into quarters, then cut each quarter into 1½-inch pieces. On four 11-inch metal skewers, evenly thread bread cubes; set aside.

3. For dressing, blend remaining ½ cup Dressing, 2 tablespoons cheese and 1 clove garlic; set aside.

4. Remove steak and red pepper from marinade, discarding marinade. On four metal skewers, alternately thread steak and red pepper. Grill, turning occasionally and brushing frequently with ⅓ cup reserved marinade, 8 to 10 minutes or until steak is medium rare to medium doneness.

5. Meanwhile, generously brush bread with remaining reserved marinade. Grill bread kabobs, turning occasionally, 4 minutes or until golden brown and toasted. To serve, toss lettuce with dressing; arrange on serving plates or platter. Top with steak, red pepper and bread. Garnish, if desired, with additional Parmesan cheese. *Makes 4 servings*

Prep Time: 20 minutes • **Marinate Time:** 30 minutes • **Cook Time:** 8 minutes

Grilled T-Bone Steaks with BBQ Rub

2 to 4 well-trimmed beef T-Bone or Porterhouse steaks, cut 1 inch thick (about 2 to 4 pounds)

BBQ RUB:
    2 tablespoons chili powder
    2 tablespoons packed brown sugar
    1 tablespoon ground cumin
    2 teaspoons minced garlic
    2 teaspoons cider vinegar
    1 teaspoon Worcestershire sauce
    ¼ teaspoon ground red pepper

1. Combine rub ingredients; press evenly onto beef steaks.

2. Place steaks on grid over medium, ash-covered coals. Grill, uncovered, 14 to 16 minutes for medium rare to medium doneness, turning occasionally. Remove bones and carve steaks into slices, if desired. Season with salt, as desired.

Makes 4 servings

Tip: To broil, place steaks on rack in broiler pan so surface of beef is 3 to 4 inches from heat. Broil 15 to 20 minutes for medium rare to medium doneness, turning once.

Prep and Cook Time: 25 minutes

Favorite recipe from **National Cattlemen's Beef Association on behalf of The Beef Checkoff**

 TIP To make grill marks for an attractive presentation, place the steak on the grid. After one minute—or halfway through the cooking time—lift the steak with tongs and rotate 90 degrees. Grill for another minute to make the crosshatch marks. Then, turn the steak over and don't flip back onto marked side again. Since only one side of the steak will show on the plate, both sides don't need crosshatches.

Greek-Style Beef Kabobs

1 pound boneless beef top sirloin steak (1 inch thick), cut into 16 pieces
¼ cup Italian salad dressing
3 tablespoons fresh lemon juice, divided
1 tablespoon dried oregano
1 tablespoon Worcestershire sauce
2 teaspoons dried basil
1 teaspoon grated lemon peel
⅛ teaspoon red pepper flakes
1 large green bell pepper, cut into 16 pieces
16 cherry tomatoes
2 teaspoons olive oil
⅛ teaspoon salt

1. Combine beef, salad dressing, 2 tablespoons lemon juice, oregano, Worcestershire, basil, lemon peel and red pepper flakes in large resealable food storage bag. Seal bag; turn to coat. Marinate in refrigerator at least 8 hours or overnight, turning occasionally.

2. Prepare grill for direct cooking.

3. Remove beef from marinade; reserve marinade. Thread four 10-inch skewers with beef, alternating with bell pepper and tomatoes. Brush kabobs with marinade. Discard remaining marinade. Grill kabobs over medium-high heat 8 to 10 minutes or to desired doneness. Transfer to serving platter.

4. Combine remaining 1 tablespoon lemon juice, olive oil and salt in small bowl. Pour mixture over kabobs.

Makes 4 servings

Prep Time: 10 minutes • **Marinate Time:** 8 hours • **Cook Time:** 5 minutes

TOOL TIP Skewers come in various shapes and sizes. Metal and wooden are the most practical. Wooden skewers are great for kabobs, and can also hold food like onion slices together. Metal skewers are often flat which keep fragile food like tofu or fish from slipping around when you turn the kabobs. Another way to hold food steady and flat when being turned is to thread it on two skewers.

Steak Parmesan

4 cloves garlic, minced
1 tablespoon coarse salt
1 tablespoon olive oil
1 teaspoon rosemary
1 teaspoon black pepper
2 beef T-bone or Porterhouse steaks, cut 1 inch thick (about 2 pounds)
¼ cup grated Parmesan cheese

1. Combine garlic, salt, oil, rosemary and pepper; press all over steaks. Let stand 15 minutes.

2. Prepare grill for direct cooking. Grill steaks, covered, over medium-high heat 15 to 20 minutes for medium-rare (145°F) or to desired doneness, turning once.

3. Transfer steaks to cutting board; sprinkle with cheese. Tent with foil; let stand 5 minutes. Serve steaks immediately. *Makes 2 to 3 servings*

 TIP For a smoky flavor, soak 2 cups hickory or oak wood chips in enough cold water to cover at least 30 minutes. Drain and scatter over hot coals before grilling.

Patio
Pork & Lamb

Spicy Hunan Ribs

1⅓ cups hoisin sauce or *Cattlemen's®* Golden Honey Barbecue Sauce
⅔ cup *Frank's® RedHot®* XTRA Hot Cayenne Pepper Sauce or *Frank's® RedHot®* Cayenne Pepper Sauce
¼ cup soy sauce
2 tablespoons brown sugar
2 tablespoons dark sesame oil
2 tablespoons grated peeled ginger root
4 cloves garlic, crushed through a press
2 full racks pork spareribs, trimmed (about 6 pounds)

1. Combine hoisin sauce, XTRA Hot Sauce, soy sauce, brown sugar, sesame oil, ginger and garlic; mix well.

2. Place ribs into large resealable plastic food storage bags. Pour 1½ cups sauce mixture over ribs. Seal bags and marinate in refrigerator 1 to 3 hours or overnight.

3. Prepare grill for indirect cooking over medium-low heat (250°F). Place ribs on rib rack or in foil pan; discard marinade. Cook on covered grill 2½ to 3 hours until very tender. Baste with remaining sauce during last 15 minutes of cooking. If desired, grill ribs over direct heat at end of cooking to char slightly. *Makes 4 to 6 servings*

Prep Time: 5 minutes • **Marinate Time:** 1 hour • **Cook Time:** 3 hours

Peachy Smothered Pork Chops

  1 tablespoon vegetable oil
  1 small onion, finely minced
  1 (12-ounce) jar peach preserves
  ⅔ cup *French's*® Honey Mustard
  2 teaspoons grated peeled ginger root
  ¼ teaspoon ground nutmeg
  6 boneless pork chops, cut 1-inch thick

1. Heat oil in small saucepan; sauté onion until tender. Stir in peach preserves, mustard, ginger and nutmeg. Heat to boiling; simmer 5 minutes or until flavors are blended. Transfer ¾ cup sauce to bowl for basting. Reserve remaining sauce; keep warm.

2. Grill or broil chops over medium direct heat 20 minutes or until barely pink in center, turning and basting often with sauce.

3. Serve chops with reserved sauce mixture.   *Makes 6 servings*

Alternate Method: Brown chops in skillet. Pour peach mixture over chops and simmer until no longer pink in center.

Prep Time: 5 minutes • **Cook Time:** 25 minutes

 TIP Basting sauces containing sugar, honey, preserves or tomato products should only be applied during the last 15 to 30 minutes of grilling to prevent charring. Also, when using sugar-based mixtures, cook over lower heat. Applying the baste for the right amount of time and at the right temperature, develops a crusty, sweet, caramelized flavor. Yum!

Pork and Plum Kabobs

¾ pound boneless pork loin chops trimmed and cut into 1-inch pieces
1½ teaspoons ground cumin
½ teaspoon ground cinnamon
¼ teaspoon salt
¼ teaspoon garlic powder
¼ teaspoon ground red pepper
¼ cup sliced green onions
¼ cup raspberry fruit spread
1 tablespoon orange juice
3 plums or nectarines, pitted and cut into wedges

1. Place pork in large resealable food storage bag. Combine cumin, cinnamon, salt, garlic powder and red pepper in small bowl; pour over pork. Seal bag; shake to coat meat with spices.

2. Combine green onions, fruit spread and orange juice in small bowl.

3. Prepare grill for direct cooking. Alternately thread pork and plum wedges onto eight skewers.* Grill kabobs over medium heat 12 to 14 minutes or until meat is cooked through, turning once during cooking. Brush frequently with raspberry mixture during last 5 minutes of grilling.

Makes 4 servings

*If using wooden skewers, soak in water 30 minutes to prevent burning.

Prep Time: 10 minutes • **Cook Time:** 12 to 14 minutes

 FOOD SAFETY TIP To avoid spreading bacteria from raw meat with the basting brush, brush the sauce on during the last 5 minutes of cooking. Always discard any remaining basting sauce.

Grilled Australian Lamb Loin Chops
with Orange-Mint Gremolata

8 Australian Lamb loin chops, trimmed
    Juice of 2 navel oranges
2 tablespoons olive oil
    Salt and freshly ground pepper, to taste

GREMOLATA
    Grated peel of 2 navel oranges
¼ cup chopped fresh mint
1 clove garlic, minced

GREEN BEANS
16 to 20 fresh green beans
1 tablespoon extra-virgin olive oil
1 tablespoon sliced almonds, toasted
    Salt and freshly ground pepper, to taste

1. Place the lamb chops in a flat glass or ceramic dish. Combine orange juice with the olive oil and pour over the lamb, turning chops to coat both sides. Season to taste with salt and pepper. Cover with plastic wrap and marinate in refrigerator for 20 to 30 minutes, turning the chops occasionally during that time.

2. To make the gremolata, combine the orange peel, mint and garlic in a small bowl and set aside.

3. Preheat grill to medium. Pat lamb dry and grill about 4 minutes on each side or until cooked as preferred. For medium rare, the chops should register 145°F on a meat thermometer or be plump and springy when pressed.

4. While the lamb is cooking, steam the beans for 1 minute or until tender-crisp. Drain the water and add the olive oil and sliced almonds. Season to taste and shake the pan gently until heated through.

5. Serve the lamb with the beans. Spoon the orange-mint gremolata over all or serve on the side.

Makes 4 servings

Prep Time: 30 minutes • **Cook Time:** 15 to 20 minutes

Favorite recipe from **Meat and Livestock Australia**

Lemon-Garlic Shish Kabobs

1½ pounds well-trimmed boneless lamb leg, cut into 1-inch pieces
¼ cup olive oil
2 tablespoons lemon juice
4 cloves garlic, minced
2 tablespoons chopped fresh oregano *or* 2 teaspoons dried oregano
½ teaspoon salt
½ teaspoon black pepper
1 red or yellow bell pepper, cut into 1-inch pieces
1 small zucchini, cut into 1-inch pieces
1 yellow squash, cut into 1-inch pieces
1 small red onion, cut into ½-inch wedges
8 ounces button mushrooms, stems trimmed

1. Place lamb in large resealable food storage bag. Combine oil, lemon juice, garlic, oregano, salt and black pepper in small bowl; pour over lamb. Seal bag; turn to coat. Marinate in refrigerator 1 to 4 hours, turning once.

2. Prepare grill for direct cooking.

3. Remove lamb from marinade; reserve marinade. Alternately thread lamb, bell pepper, zucchini, yellow squash, onion and mushrooms onto twelve 10-inch skewers.* Brush all sides with reserved marinade; discard remaining marinade.

4. Grill kabobs, covered, over medium-high heat 10 to 13 minutes or to desired doneness, turning occasionally.

Makes 6 servings

*If using wooden skewers, soak in water 30 minutes to prevent burning.

 TIP To cook kabobs to perfection, cut the pieces of food the same size to ensure the ingredients will cook evenly.

Mojo Pork Chops with Black Magic Citrus Salsa

6 boneless pork chops, ¾ inch thick (about 1½ pounds)
2 tablespoons olive oil
2 tablespoons lime juice
2 tablespoons orange juice
2 tablespoons minced garlic
½ teaspoon salt, divided
½ teaspoon red pepper flakes
2 small seedless oranges, peeled and chopped
1 medium cucumber, peeled, seeded and chopped
2 tablespoons diced red bell pepper
2 tablespoons chopped onion
2 tablespoons chopped fresh cilantro

1. Place pork in large resealable food storage bag. Add oil, lime juice, orange juice, garlic, ¼ teaspoon salt and red pepper flakes. Seal bag; turn to coat. Marinate in refrigerator at least 2 hours or up to 24 hours.

2. To make salsa, combine oranges, cucumber, bell pepper, onion and cilantro in small bowl; toss lightly. Cover and refrigerate 1 hour or overnight. Add remaining ¼ teaspoon salt just before serving.

3. Prepare grill for direct cooking. Remove pork from marinade; discard marinade. Grill pork, covered, over medium heat 8 to 12 minutes to 145°F or to desired doneness. Serve with salsa.

Makes 4 to 6 servings

Jamaican Baby Back Ribs

2 tablespoons sugar
2 tablespoons lemon juice
1 tablespoon salt
1 tablespoon vegetable oil
2 teaspoons black pepper
2 teaspoons dried thyme
¾ teaspoon ground cinnamon,
¾ teaspoon ground nutmeg
¾ teaspoon ground allspice
½ teaspoon ground red pepper
6 pounds pork baby back ribs, well trimmed and cut into 3- to 4-rib portions
Barbecue Sauce (recipe follows)

1. Combine sugar, lemon juice, salt, oil, black pepper, thyme, cinnamon, nutmeg, allspice and red pepper in small bowl; mix well. Press seasoning all over ribs. Cover; refrigerate overnight.

2. Prepare Barbecue Sauce. Prepare grill for indirect cooking.

3. Place ribs on grid directly over drip pan. Grill, covered, over medium-low heat 1 hour, turning occasionally. Baste ribs generously with Barbecue Sauce; grill 30 to 60 minutes more or until ribs are tender and browned, turning occasionally.

4. Bring remaining Barbecue Sauce to a boil in small saucepan over high heat; boil at least 1 minute. Serve ribs with heated sauce.

Makes 6 servings

Barbecue Sauce

2 tablespoons butter
½ cup finely chopped onion
1½ cups ketchup
1 cup red currant jelly
¼ cup apple cider vinegar
1 tablespoon soy sauce
¼ teaspoon ground red pepper
¼ teaspoon black pepper

Melt butter in medium saucepan over medium-high heat. Add onion; cook and stir 5 minutes or until softened. Stir in remaining ingredients. Reduce heat to medium-low; simmer 20 minutes, stirring often.

Makes about 3 cups

Mixed Grill Kabobs

  1 pound boneless beef sirloin, cut into 1-inch cubes
  2 large red, orange or yellow bell peppers, cut into chunks
12 strips bacon, blanched*
12 ounces smoked sausage or kielbasa, cut into ½-inch slices
  1 cup red pearl onions, peeled or red onion chunks
  1 pound pork tenderloin, cut lengthwise in half, then into long ¼-inch wide strips**
  1 cup pineapple wedges
1½ cups *Cattlemen's*® Award Winning Classic Barbecue Sauce

*To blanch bacon, place bacon strips into boiling water for 1 minute. Drain thoroughly.

**To easily cut pork, freeze about 30 minutes until very firm.

1. Arrange beef cubes and 1 bell pepper on metal skewers, weaving bacon strips around all. Place sausage, 1 pepper and onions on separate skewers. Ribbon strips of pork on additional skewers with pineapple wedges.

2. Baste the different kabobs with some of the barbecue sauce. Cook on a well-greased grill over medium-high direct heat, basting often with remaining barbecue sauce. Do not baste during last 5 minutes of cooking.

3. Serve a trio of kabobs to each person with additional sauce that has not been used for basting.

Makes 6 to 8 servings

Substitution: You may substitute *Cattlemen's*® Authentic Smoke House or Golden Honey Barbecue Sauce.

Prep Time: 20 minutes • **Cook Time:** 10 to 15 minutes

 FOOD SAFETY TIP Wash all utensils, cutting boards and containers with hot soapy water after they have been in contact with raw meat. Always serve cooked food from the grill on a clean plate, not the one that held the raw food.

BBQ Pulled Pork with Cola BBQ Sauce

    1 tablespoon seasoned salt
    1 tablespoon brown sugar
    ½ teaspoon ground black pepper
    1 (7-pound) Boston butt (bone-in pork shoulder roast)
      Cola BBQ Sauce (recipe follows)
      Hamburger buns

1. Combine seasoned salt, sugar and pepper. Rub mixture into pork. Place meat into large resealable plastic food storage bag. Refrigerate 3 hours. Meanwhile, prepare Cola BBQ Sauce; reserve.

2. Transfer pork to rack in disposable foil pan. Add enough water to just cover rack. Prepare grill for indirect heat, setting temperature to medium/medium-low (300°F). Cook pork in pan on covered grill for 4 to 6 hours until internal temperature reaches 195°F and meat is fall-off-the-bone tender. Transfer to cutting board and let rest 15 minutes.

3. Wearing clean rubber gloves, remove and discard fat and bone. Tear meat into long shreds, or chop coarsely, if desired. In saucepan, heat 4 cups shredded meat with 2 cups Cola BBQ Sauce. Serve on hamburger buns.

Makes 14 cups pulled pork

Prep Time: 10 minutes • **Marinate Time:** 3 hours • **Cook Time:** 4 to 6 hours

Cola BBQ Sauce

    2 tablespoons butter or vegetable oil
    1 medium onion, finely chopped
    1 clove garlic, minced
    1½ cups *Cattlemen's®* Award Winning Classic Barbecue Sauce or *Cattlemen's®*
        Authentic Smoke House Barbecue Sauce
    1 (12-ounce) can cola soda
    ⅓ cup *French's®* Worcestershire Sauce

1. Melt butter in large skillet. Add onion and garlic; cook 5 minutes over medium heat just until tender.

2. Add remaining ingredients. Heat to boiling. Reduce heat; simmer, uncovered, 25 minutes until sauce reduces to 2 cups, stirring occasionally.

Makes about 2 cups

Santa Fe Salad with Grilled Pork Tenderloin

1 whole pork tenderloin, about 1 pound
2 tablespoons Southwestern-style rub*
6 cups chopped leaf lettuce
1 (15½-ounce) can black beans, rinsed and drained
1 (12-ounce) can corn, drained
1 (7-ounce) jar roasted sweet red peppers, drained and cut into strips
½ red onion, thinly sliced
4 tablespoons olive oil
2 tablespoons fruit vinegar
1 tablespoon honey
½ teaspoon crushed red pepper flakes
   Salt, to taste
   Fresh cilantro sprigs

*Use purchased blend or combine 1 tablespoon chili powder, 1 teaspoon cumin and 1 teaspoon oregano.

Rub all surfaces of pork tenderloin with rub. Grill over medium-hot fire for about 20 minutes, turning occasionally, until internal temperature, read with meat thermometer, is 145°F. Let tenderloin rest.

Meanwhile, on each of four dinner plates arrange a bed of chopped lettuce. Divide beans, corn, roasted peppers and onion and arrange on top of lettuce.

In small bowl, stir together oil, vinegar, honey, red pepper and salt for dressing.

Slice tenderloin and divide equally; arrange slices on top of salads. Drizzle dressing over salads and garnish with cilantro.   *Makes 4 servings*

Favorite recipe from **National Pork Board**

Herbed Lamb Chops

⅓ cup vegetable oil
⅓ cup red wine vinegar
2 tablespoons soy sauce
1 tablespoon lemon juice
3 cloves garlic, crushed
1 teaspoon salt
1 teaspoon chopped fresh oregano *or* ¼ teaspoon dried oregano
1 teaspoon dried rosemary
1 teaspoon dry mustard
½ teaspoon white pepper
8 lamb loin chops (about 2 pounds), cut 1 inch thick

1. Combine all ingredients except lamb in large resealable food storage bag. Reserve ½ cup marinade for basting. Add lamb. Seal bag; turn to coat. Marinate in refrigerator at least 1 hour.

2. Prepare grill for direct cooking.

3. Remove lamb from marinade; discard marinade. Grill lamb over medium-high heat about 8 minutes or to desired doneness, turning once and basting often with reserved ½ cup marinade. Do not baste during last 5 minutes of cooking. Discard any remaining marinade.

Makes 4 to 6 servings

Creamy Cuban Mojo Pork Grill

1 cup HELLMANN'S® or BEST FOODS® Real Mayonnaise
2 cloves garlic, finely chopped
1 small jalapeño pepper, seeds and ribs removed then finely chopped
2 tablespoons orange juice
1 tablespoon lime juice
½ teaspoon ground cumin
8 pork chops

1. In medium bowl, combine all ingredients except chops. Reserve ½ cup mayonnaise mixture.

2. Season chops, if desired, with salt and ground black pepper. Grill or broil chops, turning once and brushing frequently with remaining mayonnaise mixture, until chops are done. Serve with reserved mayonnaise mixture.

Makes 8 servings

Prep Time: 10 minutes • **Cook Time:** 12 minutes

Herbed Lamb Chops

Marinated Italian Sausage and Peppers

½ cup olive oil
¼ cup red wine vinegar
2 tablespoons chopped fresh parsley
1 tablespoon dried oregano
2 cloves garlic, crushed
1 teaspoon salt
1 teaspoon black pepper
4 hot or sweet Italian sausage links
1 large onion, cut into rings
1 large bell pepper, cut into quarters
Horseradish-Mustard Spread (recipe follows)

1. Combine oil, vinegar, parsley, oregano, garlic, salt and black pepper in small bowl. Place sausages, onion and bell pepper in large resealable food storage bag; pour oil mixture into bag. Seal bag; turn to coat. Marinate in refrigerator 1 to 2 hours.

2. Prepare Horseradish-Mustard Spread; set aside. Prepare grill for direct cooking.

3. Remove sausages, onion and bell pepper from marinade; reserve marinade. Grill sausages, covered, over medium heat 4 to 5 minutes. Turn sausages and place onion and bell pepper on grid. Brush sausages and vegetables with reserved marinade; discard remaining marinade. Grill, covered, 5 minutes more or until sausage is cooked through and vegetables are crisp-tender, turning once.

4. Serve sausages and vegetables with Horseradish-Mustard Spread.   *Makes 4 servings*

Horseradish-Mustard Spread

3 tablespoons mayonnaise
1 tablespoon chopped fresh parsley
1 tablespoon prepared horseradish
1 tablespoon Dijon mustard
2 teaspoons garlic powder
1 teaspoon black pepper

Combine all ingredients in small bowl; mix well.   *Makes about ¼ cup*

Mojo Pork with Orange-Apple Salsa

1 tablespoon minced garlic
2 tablespoons olive oil
½ cup *Frank's® RedHot® Chile 'n Lime™* Hot Sauce
½ cup orange juice
2 tablespoons grated orange zest
¼ cup minced fresh cilantro
2 tablespoons chili powder
1 teaspoon dried oregano
2 boneless pork tenderloins (2 pounds)
½ cup sour cream
Orange-Apple Salsa (recipe follows)

1. Sauté garlic in oil; cool. Slowly stir in *Chile 'n Lime™* Hot Sauce, orange juice, zest, cilantro, chili powder and oregano. Reserve ¼ cup marinade.

2. Place pork into resealable plastic food storage bags. Pour remaining marinade over pork. Seal bags; marinate in refrigerator 1 to 3 hours. Combine reserved marinade with sour cream; set aside in refrigerator.

3. Grill pork over medium-high direct heat for 30 minutes or until center is no longer pink. Slice pork and drizzle with spicy sour cream. Serve with Orange-Apple Salsa.

Makes 6 to 8 servings

Note: The word "mojo" comes from the Spanish word *mojado*, which means "wet." Found predominantly in Spanish and Cuban cuisines, mojos are used as sauces or marinades.

Prep Time: 15 minutes • **Marinate Time:** 1 hour • **Cook Time:** 35 minutes

Orange-Apple Salsa

3 navel oranges, peeled, sectioned and cut into small pieces
2 large apples, cored and diced
2 tablespoons chopped red onion
2 tablespoons chopped fresh cilantro
2 tablespoons *Frank's® RedHot® Chile 'n Lime™* Hot Sauce

Combine ingredients in bowl; chill until ready to serve.

Makes about 3 cups

Glazed Ham and Sweet Potato Kabobs

1 large sweet potato (12 ounces), peeled and cut into 16 pieces
¼ cup water
1 ham slice (12 ounces), ¼ inch thick
¼ cup (½ stick) butter
¼ cup packed dark brown sugar
2 tablespoons cider vinegar
2 tablespoons molasses
1 tablespoon Worcestershire sauce
1 tablespoon yellow mustard
¾ teaspoon ground cinnamon
½ teaspoon ground allspice
⅛ teaspoon red pepper flakes
16 fresh pineapple chunks (about 1 inch)

1. Place sweet potato in shallow microwavable dish; add water. Cover; microwave on HIGH 4 minutes or until fork-tender. Drain; cool about 5 minutes.

2. Cut ham into 20 (1-inch) pieces; set aside.

3. Combine butter, brown sugar, vinegar, molasses, Worcestershire, mustard, cinnamon, allspice and red pepper flakes in medium saucepan. Bring to a boil over medium-high heat; boil 2 minutes or until sauce reduces to ½ cup. Remove from heat; cool.

4. Prepare grill for direct cooking.

5. Thread ham, sweet potato and pineapple onto four 12-inch skewers,* beginning and ending with ham.

6. Grill skewers over medium heat 6 to 8 minutes or until potatoes are browned and ham is heated through, turning every 2 minutes and brushing with sauce.   *Makes 4 servings*

*If using wooden skewers, soak in water 30 minutes to prevent burning.

Just for Fun: Toast 6 to 8 large marshmallows on skewers alongside the kabobs. Top the sweet potatoes with warm marshmallows.

Maple Francheezies

Mustard Spread (recipe follows)
¼ cup maple syrup
2 teaspoons garlic powder
1 teaspoon black pepper
½ teaspoon ground nutmeg
4 slices bacon
4 jumbo hot dogs
4 hot dog buns, split
½ cup (2 ounces) shredded Cheddar cheese

1. Prepare Mustard Spread; set aside.

2. Prepare grill for direct cooking.

3. Combine maple syrup, garlic powder, pepper and nutmeg in small bowl. Brush syrup mixture onto bacon slices. Wrap one bacon slice around each hot dog.

4. Brush hot dogs with remaining syrup mixture. Grill hot dogs, covered, over medium-high heat 8 minutes or until bacon is crisp and hot dogs are heated through, turning once. Place hot dogs in buns; top with Mustard Spread and cheese.   *Makes 4 servings*

Mustard Spread

½ cup yellow mustard
1 tablespoon finely chopped onion
1 tablespoon diced tomato
1 tablespoon chopped fresh parsley
1 teaspoon garlic powder
½ teaspoon black pepper

Combine all ingredients in small bowl; mix well.   *Makes about ¾ cup*

Margarita Pork Kabobs

1 cup margarita drink mix *or* 1 cup lime juice, 4 teaspoons sugar and
   ½ teaspoon salt
1 teaspoon ground coriander
1 clove garlic, minced
1 pound pork tenderloin, cut into 1-inch cubes
2 tablespoons margarine, melted
1 tablespoon minced fresh parsley
2 teaspoons lime juice
⅛ teaspoon sugar
1 large green or red bell pepper, cut into 1-inch cubes
2 ears corn, cut into 8 pieces

For marinade, combine margarita mix, coriander and garlic in small bowl. Place pork cubes in large resealable plastic food storage bag; pour marinade over pork. Close bag securely; turn to coat. Marinate for at least 30 minutes in refrigerator. Combine margarine, parsley, lime juice and sugar in small bowl; set aside. Thread pork cubes onto four skewers, alternating with pieces of bell pepper and corn. (If using bamboo skewers, soak in water 20 to 30 minutes before using to prevent them from burning.) Grill over hot coals for 15 to 20 minutes or until barely pink in center, basting with margarine mixture and turning frequently. *Makes 4 servings*

Favorite recipe from **National Pork Board**

 TIP When preparing kabobs, thread the ingredients loosely on the skewers. The food will cook faster and more evenly. Make additional skewers if the all the food does not fit on the number of skewers called for in the recipe.

Thai Curry Coconut Pork Chops

  1 tablespoon vegetable oil
¼ cup *each* minced green onion and yellow onion
½ cup *Cattlemen's®* Golden Honey Barbecue Sauce
½ cup cream of coconut (not coconut milk)
¼ cup *Frank's® RedHot® Chile 'n Lime™* Hot Sauce
  2 teaspoons grated peeled ginger root
½ teaspoon curry powder
¼ cup heavy cream
  6 rib cut bone-in pork chops, cut 1-inch thick, seasoned with salt
      and pepper to taste

1. Prepare Thai Curry Coconut Sauce: Heat oil in small saucepan; sauté onions just until tender. Add barbecue sauce, cream of coconut, *Chile 'n Lime™* Hot Sauce, ginger and curry powder. Simmer 5 minutes until slightly thickened. Transfer ¾ cup sauce to bowl for basting. Add cream to remaining sauce. Simmer 3 minutes; keep warm.

2. Grill chops over medium direct heat 25 minutes or until no longer pink near bone, basting with chile sauce mixture during last 10 minutes of cooking.

3. Arrange chops on serving platter. Serve with Thai Curry Coconut Sauce and, if desired, steamed jasmine rice.   *Makes 6 servings*

Serving Suggestion: For a colorful presentation, toss cooked the rice with minced red onion and parsley.

Prep Time: 5 minutes • **Cook Time:** 30 minutes

 TIP Don't walk away from the grill while cooking and watch food carefully. The total cooking time will vary with the type of food and its position on the grill, the weather, the temperature of the coals and the degree of doneness you desire. If you have to walk away, set a timer to remind you when it's time to check the food.

Grilled Pork & Pineapple Ramen Salad

½ cup reduced-sodium teriyaki sauce
¼ cup *French's®* Honey Mustard or *French's®* Honey Dijon Mustard
2 tablespoons rice vinegar
2 tablespoons peanut oil
1 tablespoon sugar
2 packages (3 ounces each) chicken-flavored ramen noodle soup
1 pound pork tenderloin
½ fresh pineapple, cored, skinned and cut into 1-inch wedges
   Chopped green onions and red bell peppers for garnish

1. Combine teriyaki sauce, mustard, vinegar, oil and sugar in glass measuring cup. Prepare ramen noodles according to package directions for soup; drain and rinse noodles. Place in large serving bowl and toss with half the dressing.

2. Grill pork over medium-high heat 20 minutes or until slightly pink in center. Grill pineapple about 5 minutes just until heated through and lightly browned. Slice pork thinly and cut pineapple into chunks.

3. Arrange pork and pineapple over noodles and drizzle with remaining dressing. Garnish with green onions and red peppers if desired.   *Makes 4 to 6 servings*

Tip: Purchase cored and skinned fresh pineapple from the produce section of the supermarket.

Prep Time: 15 minutes • **Cook Time:** 25 minutes

 TOOL TIPS A standard kitchen timer reminds you when well-done is about to become overdone when cooking foods on the grill. An instant-read thermometer is the other most valuable tool to determine just the right doneness for grilled meats and poultry.

Italian Sausage & Pepper Pita Wraps

1 cup prepared marinara sauce
½ teaspoon dried basil
¼ teaspoon dried oregano
4 (6-inch) hot or mild Italian sausage links (about 1¼ pounds)
1 green bell pepper, cut lengthwise into quarters
1 small onion, sliced
4 pita bread rounds
1 tablespoon olive oil
1 cup (4 ounces) shredded Italian cheese blend or mozzarella cheese

1. Combine marinara sauce, basil and oregano in small saucepan. Cook over medium-low heat about 5 minutes; keep warm.

2. Prepare grill for direct cooking. Place sausage links on grid; arrange bell pepper and onion around sausages. Grill, covered, over medium heat 7 minutes. Turn sausages and vegetables; grill 8 to 10 minutes or until sausages are cooked through and vegetables are crisp-tender.

3. Brush one side of pitas with oil. Place on grid; grill until soft.

4. Cut sausages in half lengthwise. Cut bell pepper into strips; separate onion slices into rings.

5. Divide sausages, bell pepper and onion among pitas. Top with sauce and cheese. Fold pitas in half. *Makes 4 servings*

 FOOD SAFETY TIP Wash your hands frequently with hot, soapy water before and after handling meat products. Antibacterial wipes come in handy for outdoor cooking away from home.

Southwestern Lamb Chops with Charred Corn Relish

    4 lamb shoulder or blade chops (about 8 ounces each), cut ¾ inch thick
    ¼ cup vegetable oil
    ¼ cup lime juice
    1 tablespoon chili powder
    2 cloves garlic, minced
    1 teaspoon ground cumin
    ¼ teaspoon ground red pepper
      Charred Corn Relish (recipe follows)
    2 tablespoons chopped fresh cilantro
      Hot pepper jelly (optional)

1. Place lamb in large resealable food storage bag. Combine oil, lime juice, chili powder, garlic, cumin and red pepper in small bowl. Reserve 3 tablespoons mixture for Charred Corn Relish; cover and refrigerate. Pour remaining mixture over lamb. Seal bag; turn to coat. Marinate in refrigerator at least 8 hours or overnight, turning occasionally.

2. Prepare grill for direct cooking. Prepare Charred Corn Relish; set aside.

3. Remove lamb from marinade; discard marinade. Grill lamb, covered, over medium heat 13 to 15 minutes for medium or to desired doneness, turning once. Sprinkle with cilantro. Serve with Charred Corn Relish and hot pepper jelly, if desired.   *Makes 4 servings*

Charred Corn Relish

    2 large ears fresh corn, husked and silk removed
    ½ cup diced red bell pepper
    ¼ cup chopped fresh cilantro
    3 tablespoons reserved lime juice mixture

1. Grill corn, covered, over medium heat 10 to 12 minutes or until charred, turning occasionally. Cool to room temperature.

2. Cut kernels off each cob into large bowl. Scrape cobs with knife to release remaining corn and liquid.

3. Add bell pepper, cilantro and reserved lime juice mixture to corn; mix well. Serve at room temperature.   *Makes about 1½ cups*

Tex-Mex Pork Kabobs with Chili Sour Cream Sauce

2¼ teaspoons chili powder, divided
1¾ teaspoons ground cumin, divided
¾ teaspoon garlic powder, divided
¾ teaspoon onion powder, divided
¾ teaspoon dried oregano, divided
1 pork tenderloin (1½ pounds), trimmed and cut into 1-inch pieces
1 cup sour cream
¾ teaspoon salt, divided
¼ teaspoon black pepper
1 large red bell pepper, seeded and cut into small chunks
1 large green bell pepper, seeded and cut into small chunks
1 large yellow bell pepper, seeded and cut into small chunks

1. Combine 1½ teaspoons chili powder, 1 teaspoon cumin, ½ teaspoon garlic powder, ½ teaspoon onion powder and ½ teaspoon oregano in medium bowl. Add pork; toss until well coated. Cover tightly; refrigerate 2 to 3 hours.

2. Combine sour cream, ¼ teaspoon salt, black pepper and remaining ¾ teaspoon chili powder, ¾ teaspoon cumin, ¼ teaspoon garlic powder, ¼ teaspoon onion powder and ¼ teaspoon oregano in small bowl; mix well. Cover tightly; refrigerate 2 to 3 hours.

3. Prepare grill for direct cooking.

4. Toss pork with remaining ½ teaspoon salt. Thread meat and bell peppers alternately onto four 10-inch skewers. Grill over medium-high heat 10 minutes or until meat is cooked through, turning several times. Serve immediately with sour cream sauce. *Makes 4 servings*

Honey-and-Garlic Australian Lamb Rack with Orzo Salad

2 racks of Australian Lamb, frenched

MARINADE
  1½ cups red wine
  2 tablespoons honey
  3 cloves garlic, crushed
  1 tablespoon fresh thyme leaves
    Salt and freshly ground pepper, to taste

ORZO SALAD
  1 pound orzo pasta
  2 ears fresh corn, cooked
    Juice and zest of 1 lemon
  2 tablespoons extra-virgin olive oil
  ¼ cup chopped black olives
  ¼ cup chopped fresh cilantro
  ¼ cup chopped fresh parsley
    Salt and freshly ground pepper, to taste

1. Combine the marinade ingredients and mix well. Pour marinade into a large flat glass or ceramic dish. Add the lamb, turning to coat all sides. Marinate, meat side down, in the refrigerator for 2 to 3 hours or overnight.

2. To make orzo salad, cook pasta according to directions on packet; drain well. While allowing orzo to cool slightly, cut kernels from fresh corn. Combine pasta, corn, juice, zest and remaining ingredients in a large bowl. Toss well; season with salt and pepper to taste.

3. Remove the meat from the marinade and pat dry. Place the marinade in a small pan and bring to a boil. It is important that the mixture comes to a rapid boil. Reduce heat and simmer until liquid starts to thicken slightly and become glossy. Keep warm. Heat grill to medium-high, and cook the lamb racks for 5 to 6 minutes each side for medium rare, or as desired. Allow to rest for 5 minutes.

4. Spoon orzo salad onto a large platter and place whole racks on top, or separate lamb into 3 to 4 chop portions and serve on individual plates. Spoon glaze over and serve with a green salad.

Makes 4 to 6 servings

Prep Time: 20 to 30 minutes • **Marinate Time:** 2 hours or overnight • **Cook Time:** 30 minutes

Favorite recipe from **Meat and Livestock Australia**

Tailgate Pizzas

1 cup pizza sauce
4 individual (8-inch) prepared pizza crusts
8 ounces Italian sausage, cooked, drained (1½ cups)
2 ounces sliced pepperoni
1 small red onion, thinly sliced
1 small red bell pepper, thinly sliced into rings
1 small green bell pepper, thinly sliced into rings
3 cups (12 ounces) shredded mozzarella cheese or Italian cheese blend
   Red pepper flakes (optional)

1. Prepare grill for indirect cooking, banking coals on sides of grill, or let coals burn down low and spread out evenly.

2. Spread pizza sauce over crusts; top with sausage, pepperoni, vegetables, cheese and red pepper flakes, if desired. Grill pizzas, covered, over low heat 8 to 10 minutes or until cheese is melted and crust is golden brown. *Makes 4 servings*

Apricot-Mustard Grilled Pork Tenderloin

1 pork tenderloin (about 1 pound)
5 tablespoons honey mustard
3 tablespoons apricot preserves

Season tenderloin with salt and pepper. In small bowl, stir together mustard and preserves. Grill pork over a medium-hot fire, brushing with mustard mixture frequently, turning once or twice until just done, about 15 minutes. *Makes 4 servings*

Favorite recipe from **National Pork Board**

Tailgate Pizzas

Barbecued Pork Loin

    1 cup apple juice
  ¼ cup soy sauce
    2 teaspoons dried rosemary
    1 teaspoon minced garlic
  ½ teaspoon lemon pepper
    1 boneless pork loin roast (3 to 3½ pounds)

1. Combine apple juice, soy sauce, rosemary, garlic and lemon pepper in small bowl; reserve ¼ cup marinade. Place pork in large resealable food storage bag; pour remaining marinade over pork. Seal bag; turn to coat. Marinate in refrigerator at least 2 hours or overnight, turning occasionally.

2. Prepare grill for direct cooking.

3. Remove pork from marinade; discard marinade. Grill pork over low heat 45 minutes or until internal temperature reaches 145°F, turning and brushing with reserved marinade. Remove pork from grill; let stand about 10 minutes before slicing. Internal temperature will continue to rise 5° to 10°F during stand time.

Makes 6 to 8 servings

Prep Time: 15 minutes • **Marinate Time:** 2 hours • **Cook Time:** 45 minutes

 TIP Larger roasts like pork loin require long, slow cooking. Try grilling over indirect heat to ensure moist and juicy meat with a delicious smoky flavor.

German Potato Salad with Grilled Sausage

⅔ cup prepared vinaigrette salad dressing

¼ cup *French's*® Spicy Brown Mustard or *French's*® Honey Dijon Mustard

1 tablespoon sugar

1½ pounds red or other boiling potatoes, cut into ¾-inch cubes

1 teaspoon salt

1 cup chopped green bell pepper

1 cup chopped celery

½ cup chopped onion

½ pound kielbasa or smoked sausage, split lengthwise

1. Combine salad dressing, mustard and sugar in large bowl; set aside.

2. Place potatoes in large saucepan. Add salt and enough water to cover potatoes. Heat to boiling. Cook 10 to 15 minutes until potatoes are tender. Drain and transfer to bowl. Add bell pepper, celery and onion. Set aside.

3. Grill sausage over medium-high heat until lightly browned and heated through. Cut into small cubes. Add to bowl with potatoes. Toss well to coat evenly. Serve warm.

Makes 6 to 8 servings

Prep Time: 15 minutes • **Cook Time:** 15 minutes

 TIP If the package of sausage is labeled fully cooked, the sausage just needs to be browned and heated through. If grilling uncooked sausage, it's best to cook the sausage in a flavorful liquid ahead of time, then finish browning on the grill. For food safety, cook sausages to an internal temperature of 145°F.

Barbecued Pork Tenderloin Sandwiches

½ cup ketchup
⅓ cup packed brown sugar
 2 tablespoons bourbon or whiskey (optional)
 1 tablespoon Worcestershire sauce
 1 clove garlic, minced
½ teaspoon dry mustard
¼ teaspoon ground red pepper
 2 whole pork tenderloins (about 1 pound each), trimmed
 1 large red onion, cut into 6 (¼-inch-thick) slices
 6 to 8 hoagie rolls or kaiser rolls, split

1. Prepare grill for direct cooking.

2. Combine ketchup, brown sugar, bourbon, if desired, Worcestershire, garlic, mustard and red pepper in small heavy saucepan with ovenproof handle; mix well. Set saucepan on one side of grid.* Simmer sauce 5 minutes or until thickened, stirring occasionally. Set aside half of sauce.

3. Grill pork, covered, over medium heat 20 minutes or until internal temperature reaches 140°F when tested with meat thermometer inserted into thickest part of pork, turning occasionally.

4. Add onion slices to grid. Brush tenderloins and onion with remaining sauce.

5. Transfer pork to cutting board; tent with foil. Let stand 10 to 15 minutes before carving. Internal temperature will continue to rise 5° to 10°F during stand time. Carve tenderloins crosswise into thin slices. Separate onion slices into rings. Divide meat and onion rings among rolls; drizzle with reserved sauce.   *Makes 6 to 8 servings*

*If desired, sauce may be prepared on stovetop. Bring sauce to a boil in medium saucepan over medium-high heat. Reduce heat to low; simmer, uncovered, 5 minutes or until thickened, stirring occasionally.

Note: If using an instant-read thermometer, do not leave in tenderloin during grilling.

Beer-Brined Grilled Pork Chops

1 bottle (12 ounces) dark beer
¼ cup packed dark brown sugar
1 tablespoon salt
1 tablespoon chili powder
2 cloves garlic, minced
3 cups cold water and ice cubes
4 pork chops (1 inch thick)

1. Whisk beer, brown sugar, salt, chili powder and garlic in medium bowl until salt is dissolved. Add ice water; stir until ice melts. Add pork chops; place plate on top to keep pork submerged in brine. Refrigerate 3 to 4 hours.

2. Prepare grill for direct cooking. Remove pork from brine; pat dry with paper towels. Grill pork, covered, over medium heat 10 to 12 minutes. Serve immediately

Makes 4 servings

 TIP Brining adds flavor and moisture to meat. Be sure that your pork chops have not been injected with a sodium solution (check the package label or ask your butcher) or they could end up too salty.

Fired-Up
Poultry

Ginger-Lime Chicken Thighs

⅓ cup vegetable oil
3 tablespoons lime juice
3 tablespoons honey
2 teaspoons grated fresh ginger *or* 1 teaspoon ground ginger
½ teaspoon red pepper flakes
6 skinless boneless chicken thighs (about 2 pounds)

1. Combine oil, lime juice, honey, ginger and red pepper flakes in small bowl; mix well. Place chicken in large resealable food storage bag. Pour ½ cup marinade over chicken; reserve remaining marinade. Seal bag; turn to coat. Marinate in refrigerator 30 to 60 minutes, turning occasionally.

2. Prepare grill for direct cooking.

3. Remove chicken from marinade; discard marinade. Grill chicken over medium-high heat 12 minutes or until internal temperature reaches 165°F when tested with meat thermometer. Brush both sides of chicken with reserved marinade during last 5 minutes of cooking.

Makes 6 servings

Spicy Barbecued Chicken

1 tablespoon paprika or smoked paprika
1 teaspoon dried thyme
½ teaspoon salt
½ teaspoon dried sage
¼ teaspoon black pepper
¼ teaspoon ground red pepper
1 broiler-fryer chicken, quartered (3½ to 4 pounds)
¾ cup ketchup
½ cup packed brown sugar
2 tablespoons soy sauce
2 tablespoons Worcestershire sauce
1 clove garlic, minced

1. Combine paprika, thyme, salt, sage, black pepper and red pepper in small bowl. Rub mixture all over chicken. Transfer chicken to large resealable food storage bag; refrigerate up to 24 hours.

2. Prepare grill for direct cooking. For basting sauce, combine ketchup, brown sugar, soy sauce, Worcestershire and garlic in small bowl; set aside.

3. Grill chicken, covered, over medium heat 30 to 40 minutes or until internal temperature reaches 165°F when tested with meat thermometer, turning once. Brush chicken generously with some of basting sauce during last 10 minutes of cooking. Serve with remaining sauce.

Makes 4 servings

 TIP Don't crowd food on the grill. It will cook more evenly with at least a ¾-inch space between the pieces.

Nancy's Grilled Turkey Meatballs

1 pound lean ground turkey breast
½ cup oats
¼ cup fresh whole wheat bread crumbs
1 egg white
3 tablespoons Parmesan cheese
2 tablespoons *French's®* Honey Dijon Mustard
¼ teaspoon crushed garlic
¼ teaspoon ground black pepper
1 cup pineapple chunks or wedges
1 small red bell pepper, cut into squares

1. Combine turkey, oats, bread crumbs, egg white, cheese, mustard, garlic and black pepper in large bowl. Mix well and form into 24 meatballs.

2. Place 4 meatballs on each skewer, alternating with pineapple and bell pepper.

3. Cook meatballs 10 minutes on well greased grill over medium heat until no longer pink inside, turning often. Serve with additional *French's®* Honey Dijon Mustard on the side for dipping.

Makes 6 servings

Tip: Combine ⅓ cup each *French's®* Honey Dijon Mustard, honey and *Frank's® RedHot®* Cayenne Pepper Sauce. Use for dipping grilled wings, ribs and chicken.

Prep Time: 15 minutes • Cook Time: 10 minutes

 TIP Ground turkey comes in various percentages of lean. Regular ground turkey (85% lean) is a combination of white and dark meat, which is comparable in fat to some lean cuts of ground beef. Ground turkey breast is lowest in fat (up to 99% lean), but it can dry out very easily when grilled. Gently form meatballs and patties to keep a light texture.

Jamaican Jerk Turkey Wraps

1½ teaspoons Caribbean jerk seasoning
1 turkey breast tenderloin (about ¾ pound)
4 cups broccoli slaw
1 large tomato, seeded and chopped (about 1⅓ cups)
⅓ cup coleslaw dressing
1 to 2 jalapeño peppers,* finely chopped
2 tablespoons prepared mustard (optional)
8 (7-inch) flour tortillas, warmed

*Jalapeño peppers can sting and irritate the skin, so wear rubber gloves when handling peppers and do not touch your eyes.

1. Prepare grill for direct cooking. Rub jerk seasoning all over turkey.

2. Combine broccoli slaw, tomato, dressing, jalapeños and mustard, if desired, in large bowl; toss gently to mix.

3. Grill turkey, covered, over medium heat 15 to 20 minutes or until internal temperature reaches 170°F when tested with meat thermometer in thickest part of tenderloin, turning occasionally. Thinly slice turkey. Serve in tortillas with broccoli slaw.   *Makes 4 servings*

 TIP To keep grilled food juicy, use tongs or a spatula when handling food on the grill. Piercing it with a fork causes delicious juices to escape and makes the food less moist.

Thai Barbecued Chicken

1 cup coarsely chopped fresh cilantro
2 jalapeño peppers, stemmed and seeded
8 cloves garlic, peeled and coarsely chopped
2 tablespoons fish sauce
1 tablespoon packed brown sugar
1 teaspoon curry powder
   Grated peel of 1 lemon
3 pounds chicken pieces

1. Combine cilantro, jalapeños, garlic, fish sauce, brown sugar, curry powder and lemon peel in food processor or blender; process until coarse paste forms.

2. Work fingers between skin and meat on breast and thigh pieces. Rub about 1 teaspoon seasoning paste under skin on each piece. Rub remaining paste all over chicken pieces. Place chicken in large resealable food storage bag or covered container; refrigerate 3 to 4 hours or overnight.

3. Prepare grill for direct cooking.

4. Grill chicken, covered, over medium heat 30 to 40 minutes or until internal temperature reaches 165°F when tested with meat thermometer, turning occasionally.   *Makes 4 servings*

 TIP Leaving the skin on chicken helps preserve its natural moisture while grilling. The skin can be easily removed before serving or at the table.

Bacon-Wrapped BBQ Chicken

8 chicken tenders, patted dry (about 1 pound)
½ teaspoon paprika or cumin
8 slices bacon
½ cup barbecue sauce

1. Prepare grill for direct cooking.

2. Sprinkle chicken strips with paprika. Wrap each chicken strip with one slice of bacon in spiral pattern.

3. Grill chicken over medium heat 6 minutes, turning occasionally. Brush with ¼ cup barbecue sauce. Grill 2 to 3 minutes more or until bacon is crisp and chicken is cooked through. Serve with remaining ¼ cup barbecue sauce.

Makes 4 servings

Grilled Chicken Tostada Salad

1 pound boneless skinless chicken breast halves
¾ cup *Frank's® RedHot® Chile 'n Lime™* Hot Sauce, divided
2 teaspoons chili powder
4 cups tortilla chips
8 cups shredded iceberg lettuce
1 cup shredded Cheddar cheese
1 cup salsa
1 cup canned or frozen, thawed whole kernel corn
½ cup sliced Spanish olives

1. Place chicken and ½ cup *Chile 'n Lime™* Hot Sauce in plastic bag. Refrigerate 20 minutes.

2. Grill chicken 10 minutes or until no longer pink in center. Slice chicken and toss with remaining *Chile 'n Lime™* Hot Sauce and chili powder.

3. Place 1 cup tortilla chips in each salad bowl. Layer remaining ingredients and chicken on top, dividing evenly among bowls. If desired, garnish with sour cream and chopped cilantro.

Makes 4 servings

Prep Time: 10 minutes • Marinate Time: 20 minutes • Cook Time: 10 minutes

Bacon-Wrapped BBQ Chicken

Grilled Sienna Chicken

¼ cup lemon juice
2 tablespoons olive oil
1 teaspoon dried basil
¾ teaspoon lemon pepper, divided
4 boneless skinless chicken breasts
1 cup diced tomatoes
½ teaspoon salt
3 cups arugula or red lettuce leaves

1. Combine lemon juice, oil, basil and ½ teaspoon lemon pepper in small bowl. Place chicken and 3 tablespoons marinade in large resealable food storage bag; reserve remaining marinade. Seal bag; turn to coat. Marinate in refrigerator 1 to 2 hours.

2. Combine tomatoes, salt and remaining ¼ teaspoon lemon pepper in small bowl; set aside. Prepare grill for direct cooking.

3. Remove chicken from marinade; discard marinade. Grill chicken, covered, over medium heat 15 to 20 minutes or until internal temperature reaches 165°F when tested with meat thermometer, turning and brushing with reserved marinade. Do not brush with marinade during last 5 minutes of cooking.

4. Slice chicken; arrange on bed of arugula. Top with tomato mixture.

Makes 4 servings

 TIP When marinating meat to boost the flavor, make sure the marinade used doesn't boost the bacteria count, too. If a marinade will also be used as a basting sauce, set aside some of the marinade ahead of time. When you're ready to grill, discard the marinade used to marinate the raw meat and use the reserved portion for basting.

Santa Fe BBQ Ranch Salad

1 cup *Cattlemen's®* Golden Honey Barbecue Sauce, divided
½ cup ranch salad dressing
1 pound boneless, skinless chicken
12 cups washed and torn Romaine lettuce
1 small red onion, thinly sliced
1 small ripe avocado, diced ½-inch
4 ripe plum tomatoes, diced ¼-inch
2 cups shredded Monterey Jack cheese
½ cup cooked, crumbled bacon

1. Prepare BBQ Ranch Dressing: Combine ½ cup barbecue sauce and salad dressing in small bowl; reserve.

2. Grill or broil chicken over medium-high heat 10 minutes until no longer pink in center. Cut into strips and toss with remaining ½ cup barbecue sauce.

3. Toss lettuce, onion, avocado, tomatoes, cheese and bacon in large bowl. Portion on salad plates, dividing evenly. Top with chicken and serve with BBQ Ranch Dressing.   *Makes 4 servings*

Tip: Serve *Cattlemen's®* Golden Honey Barbecue Sauce as a dipping sauce with chicken nuggets or seafood kabobs.

Prep Time: 15 minutes • Cook Time: 10 minutes

 FOOD SAFETY TIP When preparing food for the grill, remember to keep raw meat, poultry and seafood separate from cooked food. It is a serious problem if you forget and start chopping salad ingredients on the same cutting board or with the same knife you used to prepare the raw chicken. This is called cross contamination and is one of the most common causes of food-borne illness.

Spiced Turkey with Fruit Salsa

1 turkey breast tenderloin (6 ounces)
2 teaspoons lime juice
1 teaspoon mesquite seasoning blend or ground cumin
½ cup frozen pitted sweet cherries, thawed and halved*
¼ cup chunky salsa

*Drained canned sweet cherries can be substituted for frozen cherries.

1. Prepare grill for direct cooking. Brush turkey with lime juice. Sprinkle with mesquite seasoning.

2. Grill turkey, covered, over medium heat 15 to 20 minutes or until internal temperature reaches 170°F when tested with meat thermometer in the thickest part of tenderloin, turning once.

3. Meanwhile, combine cherries and salsa. Thinly slice turkey. Serve with salsa.

Makes 2 servings

Bistro Burgers with Blue Cheese

1 pound ground turkey or beef
¼ cup chopped fresh parsley
2 tablespoons minced chives
¼ teaspoon dried thyme leaves
2 tablespoons *French's®* Honey Dijon Mustard
    Lettuce and tomato slices
4 crusty rolls, split in half
2 ounces blue cheese, crumbled
1⅓ cups *French's®* French Fried Onions

1. In large bowl, gently mix meat, herbs and mustard. Shape into 4 patties.

2. Grill or broil patties 10 minutes or until no longer pink in center. Arrange lettuce and tomatoes on bottom half of rolls. Place burgers on top. Sprinkle with blue cheese and French Fried Onions. Cover with top half of rolls. Serve with additional mustard.

Makes 4 servings

Tip: Toast onions in microwave 1 minute for extra crispness.

Prep Time: 10 minutes • Cook Time: 10 minutes

Spiced Turkey with Fruit Salsa

Sundance Sandwich

4 boneless skinless chicken breast halves (1¼ pounds)
1 cup NEWMAN'S OWN® Balsamic Vinaigrette Salad Dressing, divided
1 red onion, sliced into 4 rounds
2 yellow bell peppers
1 Ciabatta loaf (Italian slipper bread) or 1 round Tuscan loaf (1 pound)
1 yellow tomato, sliced
1 red tomato, sliced
8 ounces whole milk fresh mozzarella, sliced
1 small bunch arugula *or* 4 romaine lettuce leaves

PESTO
1 cup packed fresh basil leaves
¼ cup pine nuts
2 cloves garlic, chopped
¼ cup olive oil
⅓ cup freshly grated Parmesan cheese
¼ teaspoon salt
⅛ teaspoon coarsely ground black pepper

Marinate chicken breasts in ¾ cup salad dressing 30 minutes. Marinate red onion rounds in remaining ¼ cup vinaigrette.

Grill or broil peppers until brown on all sides; put in paper bag until skins peel off easily, about 15 minutes. Skin and remove seeds. Cut each in quarters.

To prepare pesto, process basil, pine nuts and garlic in food processor until finely chopped. Add olive oil until blended; add cheese, salt and black pepper.

Cook chicken breasts using grill pan or barbecue over medium-high heat. Cook onion rounds with chicken 10 to 12 minutes, turning once. Thinly slice cooked chicken.

To serve, cut Ciabatta loaf horizontally in half. Spread pesto on cut sides of loaf. Layer yellow and red tomatoes, bell peppers, onions, mozzarella cheese, chicken breast slices and arugula on bread.

Makes 6 servings

Glazed Chicken & Vegetable Skewers

12 small red or new potatoes, about 1½ inches in diameter (1 pound)
   Golden Glaze (recipe follows)
 1 pound boneless skinless chicken thighs or breasts, cut into 1-inch pieces
 1 red bell pepper, cut into 1-inch pieces
 ½ small red onion, cut into 1-inch pieces

1. Place potatoes in large saucepan with enough water to cover. Bring to a boil over medium-high heat; cook about 10 minutes or until almost tender. (Or microwave on HIGH 3 to 4 minutes or until almost tender.) Drain; rinse under cold water to stop cooking.

2. Prepare Golden Glaze. Prepare grill for direct cooking. Alternately thread chicken, potatoes, bell pepper and onion onto eight 12-inch metal skewers. Brush glaze all over chicken and vegetables. Discard remaining glaze.

3. Grill skewers, covered, over medium-high heat 10 to 15 minutes or until chicken is cooked through, turning occasionally.   *Makes 4 servings*

Golden Glaze

 ¼ cup apricot or peach preserves
 2 tablespoons spicy brown mustard*
 2 cloves garlic, minced

*Dijon mustard can be substituted. Add ¼ teaspoon hot pepper sauce to glaze.

Combine all ingredients; mix well. Store tightly covered in refrigerator up to 2 weeks.
                                                                       Makes about ⅓ cup

Rustic Texas-Que Pizza

2 cups shredded cooked chicken (about 1 pound uncooked)

¼ cup *Frank's® RedHot® Chile 'n Lime™* Hot Sauce or *Frank's® RedHot®* Buffalo Wing Sauce

1 pound prepared pizza or bread dough (thawed, if frozen)

1 cup *Cattlemen's®* Award Winning Classic Barbecue Sauce

2 ripe plum tomatoes, diced

½ cup finely diced red onion

½ cup sliced black olives (2.25 ounce can)

2 cups shredded taco blend cheese

Cilantro or green onions, minced (optional)

1. Toss chicken with *Chile 'n Lime™* Hot Sauce; set aside. Divide dough in half. Gently stretch or roll each piece of dough into 13×9-inch rectangle on floured surface. Coat one side with vegetable cooking spray.

2. Cook dough, coated side down, on greased grill over medium-high heat for 5 minutes until browned and crisp on bottom. Using tongs, turn dough over. Spread each pizza crust with barbecue sauce and top with chicken mixture, tomatoes, onion, olives and cheese, dividing evenly.

3. Grill pizzas about 5 minutes longer until bottom is browned, crispy and cheese melts. Garnish with minced cilantro or green onions, if desired.

Makes 8 servings

Variation: Top pizza with different shredded cheeses, such as Cheddar or Jack, or with other vegetables, such as whole kernel corn, jalapeño or bell peppers.

Tip: For easier handling, allow pizza dough to rest 30 minutes in an oiled, covered bowl at room temperature.

Prep Time: 15 minutes • Cook Time: 10 minutes

Mediterranean Chicken Kabobs

2 pounds boneless skinless chicken breasts or chicken tenders, cut into 1-inch pieces
1 small eggplant, peeled and cut into 1-inch pieces
1 medium zucchini, cut crosswise into ½-inch slices
2 medium onions, each cut into 8 wedges
16 medium mushrooms, stemmed
16 cherry tomatoes
1 cup chicken broth
⅔ cup balsamic vinegar
3 tablespoons olive oil
2 tablespoons dried mint
4 teaspoons dried basil
1 tablespoon dried oregano
2 teaspoons grated lemon peel
   Chopped fresh parsley
4 cups hot cooked couscous

1. Alternately thread chicken, eggplant, zucchini, onions, mushrooms and tomatoes onto 16 metal skewers; place in large glass baking dish.

2. Combine broth, vinegar, oil, mint, basil and oregano in small bowl; pour over kabobs. Cover and marinate in refrigerator 2 hours, turning occasionally.

3. Spray grid with nonstick cooking spray. Prepare grill for direct cooking. Remove kabobs from marinade; discard marinade. Grill kabobs, covered, over medium-high heat 10 to 15 minutes or until chicken is cooked through, turning once.

4. Stir lemon peel and parsley into couscous; serve with kabobs.   *Makes 8 servings*

 TIP These kabobs can be broiled instead of grilled. Preheat the broiler. Broil the kabobs 6 inches from heat 10 to 15 minutes or until the chicken is cooked through, turning kabobs once.

Lime-Mustard Marinated Chicken

2 boneless skinless chicken breasts
¼ cup fresh lime juice
3 tablespoons honey mustard, divided
1 tablespoon olive oil
¼ teaspoon ground cumin
⅛ teaspoon garlic powder
⅛ teaspoon ground red pepper
¾ cup plus 2 tablespoons chicken broth, divided
¼ cup uncooked rice
1 cup broccoli florets
⅓ cup matchstick carrots

1. Place chicken in large resealable food storage bag. Whisk lime juice, 2 tablespoons mustard, olive oil, cumin, garlic powder and red pepper. Pour over chicken. Seal bag; turn to coat. Marinate in refrigerator 2 hours.

2. Combine ¾ cup broth, rice and remaining 1 tablespoon mustard in small saucepan. Bring to a boil over high heat. Reduce heat to medium. Cover; simmer 12 minutes or until rice is almost tender. Stir in broccoli, carrots and remaining 2 tablespoons broth. Cook, covered, 2 to 3 minutes or until vegetables are crisp-tender and rice is tender.

3. Meanwhile, prepare grill for direct cooking. Remove chicken from marinade; discard marinade. Grill chicken, covered, over medium heat 10 to 13 minutes or until internal temperature reaches 165°F when tested with meat thermometer, turning once. Serve chicken with rice mixture.

Makes 2 servings

BBQ Glazed Turkey a la Orange

1 whole turkey (12 to 14 pounds)
2 tablespoons olive oil
    Salt and black pepper to taste
1 orange, cut into quarters
6 sprigs fresh thyme
2 large disposable aluminum foil pans
    Honey BBQ Orange Glaze (recipe follows)

1. Rub turkey with oil; season with salt and pepper to taste. Place orange and thyme into cavity. Tie legs together and tuck wing tips underneath. Place turkey on rack in doubled foil pan. Set on grill.

2. Grill turkey, covered, over indirect medium heat (325°F) for 11 to 14 minutes per pound or until meat thermometer inserted into turkey thigh reaches 180°F. Baste turkey with some of the Honey BBQ Orange Glaze during last 30 minutes of cooking. Reserve remaining glaze.

3. Remove turkey to platter. Discard orange and thyme from cavity. Loosely tent with foil and let rest 15 minutes before carving. Heat reserved Honey BBQ Orange Glaze and serve with turkey.

Makes 8 servings

Prep Time: 10 minutes • Cook Time: 2½ to 3½ hours

Honey BBQ Orange Glaze

1 cup *Cattlemen's*® Golden Honey Barbecue Sauce
¼ cup orange-flavor liqueur or orange juice
¼ cup butter
1 tablespoon grated orange zest
2 teaspoons minced fresh thyme leaves

Place all ingredients in small saucepan. Simmer until butter melts, flavors are blended and sauce thickens slightly.

Makes about 1½ cups

Grilled Chicken with Chimichurri Salsa

4 boneless skinless chicken breasts
¼ cup plus 4 teaspoons olive oil, divided
½ teaspoon salt
¼ teaspoon black pepper
½ cup finely chopped parsley
¼ cup white wine vinegar
2 tablespoons finely chopped onion
3 cloves garlic, minced
1 jalapeño pepper,* finely chopped
2 teaspoons dried oregano

*Jalapeño peppers can sting and irritate the skin, so wear rubber gloves when handling peppers and do not touch your eyes.

1. Prepare grill for direct cooking.

2. Brush chicken with 4 teaspoons oil; season with salt and black pepper. Grill chicken, covered, over medium heat 10 to 16 minutes or until internal temperature reaches 165°F when tested with meat thermometer, turning once.

3. For salsa, combine parsley, remaining ¼ cup oil, vinegar, onion, garlic, jalapeño, oregano, salt and black pepper. Serve over chicken.

Makes 4 servings

Tip: Chimichurri salsa has a fresh, green color. Serve it with grilled steak or fish as well as chicken. Chimichurri will remain fresh tasting for 24 hours.

 FOOD SAFETY TIP All frozen foods should be thawed in the refrigerator, not at room temperature, before grilling. If you use the microwave to speed up thawing, grill the food immediately.

Jamaican Chicken Sandwich

1 teaspoon Jerk Seasoning (recipe follows)
4 boneless skinless chicken breasts
2 tablespoons mayonnaise
2 tablespoons plain yogurt
1 tablespoon mango chutney
4 onion rolls, split and toasted
4 lettuce leaves
8 slices peeled mango or papaya

1. Prepare Jerk Seasoning. Sprinkle 1 teaspoon seasoning all over chicken.

2. Prepare grill for direct cooking.

3. Grill chicken, covered, 10 to 14 minutes over medium heat or until internal temperature reaches 165°F when tested with meat thermometer, turning once. Meanwhile, combine mayonnaise, yogurt and chutney in small bowl.

4. Serve chicken on rolls with mayonnaise mixture, lettuce and mango slices.

Makes 4 servings

Prep Time: 8 minutes • Cook Time: 14 minutes

Jerk Seasoning

1½ teaspoons salt
1½ teaspoons ground allspice
1 teaspoon sugar
1 teaspoon ground thyme
1 teaspoon black pepper
½ teaspoon garlic powder
½ teaspoon ground red pepper
¼ teaspoon ground cinnamon
¼ teaspoon ground nutmeg

Combine all ingredients in small bowl. Store in a tightly covered container.

Makes about 2 tablespoons

Chicken Kabobs with Thai Dipping Sauce

1 pound boneless skinless chicken breasts, cut into 1-inch cubes
1 small cucumber, seeded and cut into 1-inch chunks
1 cup cherry tomatoes
2 green onions, cut into 1-inch pieces
⅔ cup teriyaki baste and glaze sauce
⅓ cup *Frank's® RedHot®* Original Cayenne Pepper Sauce
⅓ cup peanut butter
3 tablespoons frozen orange juice concentrate, undiluted
2 cloves garlic, minced

1. Thread chicken, cucumber, tomatoes and onions alternately onto metal skewers; set aside.

2. To prepare Thai Dipping Sauce, combine teriyaki baste and glaze sauce, *Frank's® RedHot®* Sauce, peanut butter, orange juice concentrate and garlic; mix well. Reserve ⅔ cup sauce for dipping.

3. Brush skewers with some of remaining sauce. Place skewers on oiled grid. Grill over hot coals 10 minutes or until chicken is no longer pink in center, turning and basting often with remaining sauce. Serve skewers with reserved Thai Dipping Sauce. Garnish as desired.

Makes 6 appetizer servings

Prep Time: 15 minutes • Cook Time: 10 minutes

Cherry Glazed Turkey Breast

1 bone-in (2½-pound) turkey breast half
½ cup cherry preserves
1 tablespoon red wine vinegar

Prepare grill for indirect-heat cooking. Place turkey, skin side up, on rack over drip pan. Cover and grill turkey breast 1 to 1¼ hours or until meat thermometer inserted in thickest portion of breast registers 170°F.

Combine preserves and vinegar in small bowl. Brush glaze on breast ½ hour before end of grilling time. Remove turkey breast from grill and let stand 15 minutes.

To serve, slice breast and arrange on platter.

Makes 6 servings

Favorite recipe from **National Turkey Federation**

Chicken Kabobs with Thai
Dipping Sauce

Garlic & Lemon Herb Marinated Chicken

 3 to 4 pounds bone-in chicken pieces, skinned if desired
⅓ cup *French's®* Honey Dijon Mustard
⅓ cup lemon juice
⅓ cup olive oil
 3 cloves garlic, minced
 1 tablespoon grated lemon zest
 1 tablespoon minced fresh thyme or rosemary
 1 teaspoon coarse salt
½ teaspoon coarse black pepper

1. Place chicken into resealable plastic food storage bag. Combine remaining ingredients. Pour over chicken. Marinate in refrigerator 1 to 3 hours.

2. Remove chicken from marinade. Grill chicken over medium direct heat for 35 to 45 minutes until juices run clear near bone (170°F for breast meat; 180°F for dark meat). Serve with additional mustard on the side. *Makes 4 servings*

Tip: This marinade is also great on whole chicken or pork chops.

Prep Time: 10 minutes • Marinate Time: 1 hour • Cook Time: 45 minutes

Grilled Chicken au Brie

 1 (5-ounce) package ALOUETTE® Crème de Brie® Original flavor
½ cup chopped walnuts, divided
 4 strips bacon, cooked crisp and crumbled
 2 tablespoons brown sugar
 4 boneless, skinless chicken breasts

Blend *Crème de Brie®*, ¼ cup of walnuts, crumbled bacon and brown sugar over low heat, stirring just until mixture thins. Grill chicken until done. Place chicken on individual serving dishes, ladle cheese sauce over chicken and sprinkle with remaining ¼ cup chopped walnuts.

Makes 4 servings

Garlic & Lemon Herb Marinated
Chicken

Buffalo Chicken Drumsticks

8 large chicken drumsticks (about 2 pounds)
3 tablespoons hot pepper sauce
1 tablespoon vegetable oil
1 clove garlic, minced
¼ cup mayonnaise
3 tablespoons sour cream
1 tablespoon white wine vinegar
¼ teaspoon sugar
⅓ cup (about 1½ ounces) crumbled Roquefort or blue cheese
2 cups hickory chips
 Celery sticks

1. Place chicken in large resealable food storage bag. Combine pepper sauce, oil and garlic in small bowl; pour over chicken. Seal bag; turn to coat. Marinate in refrigerator at least 1 hour or up to 24 hours for hotter flavor, turning occasionally.

2. For blue cheese dressing, combine mayonnaise, sour cream, vinegar and sugar in another small bowl. Stir in cheese; cover and refrigerate.

3. Cover hickory chips with cold water; soak 20 minutes. Prepare grill for direct cooking. Remove chicken from marinade; discard marinade. Drain hickory chips; sprinkle over coals. Grill, covered, over medium-hot coals 25 to 30 minutes or until chicken is tender when pierced with fork and no longer pink near bone, turning occasionally. Serve with blue cheese dressing and celery sticks.

Makes 4 servings

Magically Moist Turkey Burgers

1¼ pounds ground turkey
½ cup finely chopped orange or red bell pepper
⅓ cup HELLMANN'S® or BEST FOODS® Real Mayonnaise
¼ cup plain dry bread crumbs
2 tablespoons finely chopped sweet onion
2 tablespoons finely chopped fresh parsley (optional)
½ teaspoon salt (optional)

In medium bowl, combine all ingredients; shape into 6 burgers. Grill or broil until done. Serve, if desired, on hamburger buns with your favorite toppings.

Makes 6 servings

Prep Time: 10 minutes • Cook Time: 10 minutes

Italian Grilled Chicken Sandwiches

1 cup WISH-BONE® Italian Dressing
1 pound boneless, skinless chicken breasts
1 small eggplant, cut into ½-inch-thick slices (about ¾ pound)
1 medium zucchini, cut diagonally into ¼-inch-thick slices (about ½ pound)
  Green leaf lettuce
1 package (8 ounces) fresh mozzarella cheese, sliced
1 jar (12 ounces) roasted red peppers packed in oil, drained
1 loaf peasant bread, sliced and grilled

1. In large, shallow nonaluminum baking dish or plastic bag, pour ¾ cup Wish-Bone Italian Dressing over chicken, eggplant and zucchini. Cover, or close bag, and marinate in refrigerator, turning occasionally, up to 3 hours.

2. Remove chicken and vegetables from marinade, discarding marinade. Grill or broil chicken and vegetables, turning once and brushing occasionally with remaining ¼ cup Dressing, until chicken is thoroughly cooked and vegetables are tender.

3. To serve, layer lettuce, hot vegetables, cheese, hot chicken and roasted peppers on bread.

Makes 4 servings

Prep Time: 15 minutes • Marinate Time: 3 hours • Cook Time: 12 minutes

FOOD SAFETY TIP To avoid cross-contamination, divide the dressing used for basting the uncooked food into two small separate bowls. Use two basting brushes—one for the chicken and one for the vegetables.

Chicken Tikka (Tandoori-Style Grilled Chicken)

2 chickens (3 pounds each), cut up
1 pint nonfat yogurt
½ cup *Frank's® RedHot®* Original Cayenne Pepper Sauce
1 tablespoon grated peeled fresh ginger
3 cloves garlic, minced
1 tablespoon paprika
1 tablespoon cumin seeds, crushed *or* 1½ teaspoons ground cumin
2 teaspoons salt
1 teaspoon ground coriander

1. Remove skin and visible fat from chicken pieces. Rinse with cold water and pat dry. Randomly poke chicken all over with tip of sharp knife. Place chicken in resealable plastic food storage bags or large glass bowl. Combine yogurt, *Frank's® RedHot®* Sauce, ginger, garlic, paprika, cumin, salt and coriander in medium bowl; mix well. Pour over chicken pieces, turning pieces to coat evenly. Seal bags or cover bowl and marinate in refrigerator 1 hour or overnight.

2. Place chicken on oiled grid, reserving marinade. Grill over medium coals 45 minutes or until chicken is no longer pink near bone and juices run clear, turning and basting often with marinade. (Do not baste during last 10 minutes of cooking.) Discard any remaining marinade. Serve warm.

Makes 6 servings

Prep Time: 15 minutes • Marinate Time: 1 hour • Cook Time: 45 minutes

 TIP Yogurt is an acidic tenderizing ingredient and ginger contains a tenderizing enzyme. Marinating with either of these ingredients longer than 24 hours will result in a mushy texture. However, both provide wonderful flavor and texture if used within the appropriate amount of time.

Turkey Ham Quesadillas

¼ cup picante sauce or salsa, plus additional for dipping
4 (7-inch) regular or whole wheat flour tortillas
½ cup (2 ounces) shredded Monterey Jack cheese
¼ cup finely chopped turkey ham or lean ham
¼ cup canned diced mild green chiles, drained *or* 1 to 2 tablespoons chopped jalapeño pepper
Sour cream

1. Spread 1 tablespoon picante sauce on each tortilla.

2. Sprinkle cheese, turkey ham and chiles evenly over half of each tortilla. Fold over uncovered half to make quesadilla; spray tops and bottoms of quesadillas with nonstick cooking spray.

3. Grill quesadillas, covered, over medium heat 1½ minutes per side or until cheese is melted and tortillas are golden brown. Serve with additional picante sauce and sour cream.

Makes 8 appetizer servings

Grilled Chicken Thighs

8 boneless, skinless chicken thighs
3 tablespoons MRS. DASH® Chicken Grilling Blend™
4 tablespoons red wine vinegar
2 tablespoons tomato paste
2 tablespoons honey
1 to 2 tablespoons water

Lay chicken thighs side-by-side in large glass casserole. Score each thigh 2 to 3 times using sharp knife.

Combine MRS. DASH® Chicken Grilling Blend™, vinegar, tomato paste, honey and water. Set aside ¼ cup. Pour remaining marinade over chicken; marinate in refrigerator at least 1 hour.

Preheat grill to medium heat.

Brush thighs with reserved marinade and grill 10 minutes on each side.

Makes 4 servings

Turkey Ham Quesadillas

Cajun BBQ Beer-Can Chicken

4 (12-ounce) cans beer or non-alcoholic malt beverage
1½ cups *Cattlemen's®* Award Winning Classic Barbecue Sauce
¾ cup Cajun spice or Southwest seasoning blend
3 whole chickens (3 to 4 pounds each)
12 sprigs fresh thyme

CAJUN BBQ SAUCE
1 cup *Cattlemen's®* Award Winning Classic Barbecue Sauce
½ cup beer or non-alcoholic malt beverage
¼ cup butter
1 tablespoon Cajun spice or Southwest seasoning blend

1. Combine 1 can beer, 1½ cups barbecue sauce and ½ cup spice blend. Following manufacturer's instructions, fill marinade injection needle with marinade. Inject chickens in several places at least 1-inch deep. Place chickens into resealable plastic food storage bags. Pour any remaining marinade over chickens. Seal bags; marinate in refrigerator 1 to 3 hours or overnight.

2. Meanwhile prepare Cajun BBQ Sauce: In saucepan, combine 1 cup barbecue sauce, ½ cup beer, butter and 1 tablespoon spice blend. Simmer 5 minutes. Refrigerate and warm just before serving.

3. Open remaining cans of beer. Spill out about ½ cup beer from each can. Using can opener, punch several holes in tops of cans. Spoon about 1 tablespoon additional spice blend and 4 sprigs thyme into each can. Place 1 can upright into each cavity of chicken, arranging legs forward so chicken stands upright.

4. Place chickens upright over indirect heat on barbecue grill. Cook on a covered grill on medium-high (350°F), about 1½ hours until thigh meat registers 165°F internal temperature. (Cover chickens with foil if they become too brown while cooking.) Let stand 10 minutes before serving. Using tongs, carefully remove cans from chicken. Cut into quarters to serve. Serve with Cajun BBQ Sauce.
    Makes 12 servings

Prep Time: 20 minutes • Marinate Time: 1 hour or overnight • Cook Time: 1½ hours

TOOL TIP Injection needles can be found at most houseware stores and in specialty cooking stores.

Teriyaki Chicken Kabobs

¾ cup teriyaki marinade
¼ cup pineapple juice
 1 teaspoon jarred minced garlic in olive oil
 1 pound boneless skinless chicken breasts, cut into 1-inch cubes
 1 medium green bell pepper, cut into 1-inch squares
 2 medium zucchini, cut into ½-inch slices
 1 small red onion, cut into ½-inch chunks
 1 teaspoon black pepper

1. Combine teriyaki marinade, pineapple juice and garlic in small bowl. Place chicken in large resealable food storage bag. Add ¾ cup marinade; reserve remaining marinade. Seal bag; turn to coat. Marinate in refrigerator 30 minutes.

2. Prepare grill for direct cooking.

3. Remove chicken from marinade; discard marinade. Alternately thread chicken, bell pepper, zucchini and onion onto six skewers.* Sprinkle with pepper. Grill kabobs, covered, over medium-high heat 10 to 15 minutes or until chicken is cooked through, turning and brushing with remaining ¼ cup marinade. Do not brush with marinade during last 5 minutes of cooking.

Makes 4 to 6 servings

*If using wooden skewers, soak in water 30 minutes to prevent burning.

Teriyaki Chicken Kabobs

Cumin BBQ Chicken

1 cup prepared barbecue sauce
½ cup orange juice
3 tablespoons vegetable oil
2 tablespoons minced garlic
2 teaspoons ground coriander
2 teaspoons ground cumin
1 teaspoon black pepper
½ teaspoon salt
2 whole chickens (about 3½ pounds each), cut up

1. Combine barbecue sauce, orange juice, oil, garlic, coriander, cumin, pepper and salt in medium bowl; mix well. Reserve ¾ cup sauce.

2. Prepare grill for direct cooking.

3. Grill chicken, covered, over medium heat 20 minutes. Brush lightly with remaining sauce. Grill about 20 minutes more or until internal temperature reaches 165°F when tested with meat thermometer. Serve with reserved ¾ cup sauce. *Makes 8 servings*

Buffalo Chicken Salad

¼ cup cayenne pepper sauce
4 tablespoons I CAN'T BELIEVE IT'S NOT BUTTER!® Spread, melted
4 boneless, skinless chicken breast halves (about 1¼ pounds)
8 cups torn red or green leaf lettuce
1 medium cucumber, thinly sliced
½ cup sliced celery
½ cup WISH-BONE® Creamy Blue Cheese with Gorgonzola Dressing

1. In small bowl, blend cayenne pepper sauce and Spread. Season, if desired, with salt.

2. Grill or broil chicken, turning once and brushing frequently with hot pepper sauce mixture, 12 minutes or until chicken is thoroughly cooked.

3. In large bowl or on serving platter, toss lettuce, cucumber, celery and Wish-Bone Creamy Blue Cheese with Gorgonzola Dressing. To serve, slice chicken and arrange over salad.
Makes 4 servings

Cumin BBQ Chicken

Jamaican Rum Chicken

6 boneless skinless chicken breasts
½ cup dark rum
2 tablespoons packed brown sugar
2 tablespoons lime juice or lemon juice
2 tablespoons soy sauce
4 cloves garlic, minced
1 to 2 jalapeño peppers,* seeded and minced
1 tablespoon minced fresh ginger
1 teaspoon dried thyme
½ teaspoon black pepper

*Jalapeño peppers can sting and irritate the skin, so wear rubber gloves when handling peppers and do not touch your eyes.

1. Place chicken in large resealable food storage bag. Combine rum, brown sugar, lime juice, soy sauce, garlic, jalapeño, ginger, thyme and black pepper in medium bowl; pour over chicken. Seal bag; turn to coat. Marinate in refrigerator 4 hours or overnight, turning bag once.

2. Prepare grill for direct cooking.

3. Remove chicken from marinade; reserve marinade. Grill chicken, covered, over medium heat 12 to 16 minutes or until internal temperature reaches 165°F when tested with meat thermometer, turning once.

4. Meanwhile, bring remaining marinade to a boil in small saucepan over medium-high heat. Boil 5 minutes or until marinade is reduced by about half. Drizzle marinade over chicken.

Makes 6 servings

Grilled Lemon Chicken Dijon

⅓ cup HOLLAND HOUSE® White with Lemon Cooking Wine
⅓ cup olive oil
2 tablespoons Dijon mustard
1 teaspoon dried thyme leaves
2 whole chicken breasts, skinned, boned and halved

In shallow baking dish combine cooking wine, oil, mustard and thyme. Add chicken and turn to coat. Cover; marinate in refrigerator for 1 to 2 hours.

Prepare grill for direct cooking. Drain chicken, reserving marinade. Grill chicken over medium coals 12 to 16 minutes or until cooked through, turning once and basting with marinade.*

Makes 4 servings

*Do not baste during last 5 minutes of grilling.

Fajita Chicken Salad

1 cup WISH-BONE® Italian Dressing, divided
1 pound boneless, skinless chicken breast halves
2 large red, green or yellow bell peppers, quartered
1 large sweet onion, quartered
4 fajita-size flour tortillas
6 cups torn romaine lettuce leaves
1 medium lime, cut into wedges (optional)

1. In large, resealable plastic bag, pour ¼ cup Wish-Bone Italian Dressing over chicken; turn to coat. In another large, resealable plastic bag, pour ¼ cup Dressing over red peppers and onion. Close bags and marinate in refrigerator up to 3 hours.

2. Remove chicken and vegetables from marinades, discarding marinades. Grill or broil chicken and vegetables, turning once and brushing frequently with remaining ½ cup Dressing, 12 minutes or until chicken is thoroughly cooked and vegetables are crisp-tender. Lightly grill tortillas, turning once and brushing with additional Dressing, if desired. Tear tortillas into bite-size pieces.

3. To serve, thinly slice chicken and vegetables. Arrange lettuce on serving platter; top with chicken, vegetables, tortillas and lime. Serve, if desired, with additional Dressing.

Makes 4 servings

Prep Time: 20 minutes • Marinate Time: up to 3 hours • Cook Time: 12 minutes

Grilled Lemon Chicken Dijon

Grilled Chicken with Chili Beer Baste

3 bottles (12 ounces each) pilsner beer, divided
½ cup tomato juice
½ cup ketchup
¼ cup Worcestershire sauce
2 tablespoons packed brown sugar
1 tablespoon lemon juice
2 teaspoons chili powder
2 chipotle peppers in adobo sauce, minced
1 teaspoon dry mustard
½ teaspoon salt
½ teaspoon black pepper
2 tablespoons vegetable oil
1 small onion, chopped
1 clove garlic, minced
2 whole chickens (about 3½ pounds each), cut up

1. For Chili Beer Baste, combine one bottle of beer, tomato juice, ketchup, Worcestershire, brown sugar, lemon juice, chili powder, chipotle peppers, mustard, salt and black pepper in medium bowl; whisk until well blended. Heat oil in large saucepan over medium heat. Add onion and garlic; cook and stir 5 minutes or until onion is tender. Add beer mixture. Bring to a simmer; cook until sauce is thickened slightly and reduced to about 2 cups. Let cool. Refrigerate overnight.

2. Place chicken pieces in two large resealable food storage bags. Pour remaining two bottles of beer over chicken in bags; seal bags. Marinate in refrigerator 8 hours or overnight.

3. Prepare grill for direct cooking. Remove chicken from marinade; discard marinade. Grill chicken, covered, over medium heat 25 to 30 minutes or until internal temperature reaches 165°F when tested with meat thermometer, turning occasionally.

4. Heat 1 cup Chili Beer Baste in small saucepan over medium heat; keep warm. Brush chicken generously with remaining Chili Beer Baste during last 10 minutes of cooking.

5. Serve chicken with warm Chili Beer Baste.

Makes 8 servings

Sizzling Seafood

Grilled Fish with Lemon Parsley Butter

6 tablespoons butter, softened
3 tablespoons finely chopped fresh parsley
1 teaspoon grated lemon peel
½ teaspoon salt
½ teaspoon dried rosemary
6 lean white fish fillets, such as grouper or snapper (6 ounces each)
   Olive oil
3 medium lemons, halved

1. Combine butter, parsley, lemon peel, salt and rosemary in small bowl; set aside.

2. Prepare grill for direct cooking.

3. Coat fish with oil. Grill fish, uncovered, over high heat 6 minutes or until center is opaque, turning once.

4. Squeeze juice from one lemon half over each fillet. Top with lemon parsley butter.

Makes 6 servings

Pineapple-Scallop Bites

½ cup *French's®* Honey Dijon Mustard
¼ cup orange marmalade
 1 cup canned pineapple cubes (24 pieces)
12 sea scallops (8 ounces), cut in half crosswise
12 strips (6 ounces) uncooked turkey bacon, cut in half crosswise*

*Or substitute regular bacon for turkey bacon. Simmer 5 minutes in enough boiling water to cover; drain well before wrapping scallops.

1. Soak 12 (6-inch) bamboo skewers in hot water 20 minutes. Combine mustard and marmalade in small bowl. Reserve ½ cup mustard mixture for dipping sauce.

2. Hold 1 pineapple cube and 1 scallop half together. Wrap with 1 bacon strip. Thread onto skewer. Repeat with remaining pineapple, scallops and bacon.

3. Place skewers on oiled grid. Grill over medium heat 6 minutes, turning frequently and brushing with remaining mustard mixture. Serve hot with reserved dipping sauce.   *Makes 6 servings*

Prep Time: 25 minutes • Cook Time: 6 minutes

 TIP Of the two types of scallops, sea scallops and bay scallops, sea scallops are better for grilling because they are larger and meatier. They cook fast, about 2 to 3 minutes per side.

Salmon Salad with Basil Vinaigrette

    Basil Vinaigrette (recipe follows)
1¼ teaspoons salt, divided
  1 pound asparagus, trimmed
  1 salmon fillet (about 1 pound)
1½ teaspoons olive oil
  ¼ teaspoon black pepper
  4 lemon wedges

1. Prepare Basil Vinaigrette. Oil grid. Prepare grill for direct cooking.

2. Place 3 inches of water and 1 teaspoon salt in large saucepan or Dutch oven. Bring to boil over high heat. Add asparagus; simmer 6 to 8 minutes or until asparagus is crisp-tender. Drain and set aside.

3. Brush salmon with oil. Sprinkle with remaining ¼ teaspoon salt and pepper. Grill salmon over medium-high heat 8 to 10 minutes or until center is opaque.

4. Remove skin from salmon. Break into bite-size pieces. Arrange salmon over asparagus spears on serving plate. Spoon Basil Vinaigrette over salmon. Serve with lemon wedges.

Makes 4 servings

Basil Vinaigrette

  3 tablespoons extra virgin olive oil
  1 tablespoon minced fresh basil
  1 tablespoon white wine vinegar
  1 teaspoon minced fresh chives
  1 clove garlic, minced
  ¼ teaspoon black pepper
  ⅛ teaspoon salt

Combine all ingredients in small bowl; whisk until blended.

Makes ¼ cup

Fish Tacos with Yogurt Sauce

SAUCE

- ½ cup plain yogurt
- Juice of 1 lime
- ¼ cup chopped fresh cilantro
- 3 tablespoons sour cream
- 1 tablespoon mayonnaise
- ½ teaspoon ground cumin
- ¼ teaspoon ground red pepper
- Salt and black pepper

TACOS

- Juice of ½ lime
- 2 tablespoons canola oil
- 1½ pounds swordfish, halibut or tilapia fillets
- ¼ teaspoon salt
- ¼ teaspoon black pepper
- 12 corn or flour tortillas
- 3 cups shredded cabbage or prepared coleslaw mixture
- 2 medium tomatoes, chopped

1. For sauce, mix yogurt, juice of 1 lime, cilantro, sour cream, mayonnaise, cumin and red pepper in small bowl. Season with salt and black pepper.

2. For tacos, combine juice of ½ lime and oil in small bowl. Brush or spoon lime mixture over fish fillets 5 minutes* before cooking. Season with salt and pepper.

3. Oil grid. Prepare grill for direct cooking. Grill fish** over medium-high heat 10 minutes or until center is opaque, turning once. Flake fish or break into large pieces.

4. Reduce heat to medium. Grill tortillas 10 seconds on each side or until beginning to bubble and brown lightly. Fill tortillas with fish. Top with sauce, cabbage and tomatoes.   *Makes 6 servings*

*Do not marinate the fish longer than 5 minutes or the acid in the lime juice will begin to "cook" the fish.

**Fish can also be cooked on the grill in a grill basket.

Caribbean Glazed Swordfish with Grilled Pineapple Chutney

½ cup *Frank's® RedHot®* Cayenne Pepper Sauce or *Frank's® RedHot®* XTRA Hot
    Cayenne Pepper Sauce
¼ cup packed light brown sugar
1 teaspoon dried thyme leaves
½ teaspoon ground allspice
2 tablespoons olive oil
4 swordfish steaks, 1-inch thick, seasoned with salt and pepper to taste
    Grilled Pineapple Chutney (recipe follows)

1. Whisk together *Frank's® RedHot®* Sauce, sugar, thyme and allspice in small bowl. Reserve 3 tablespoons mixture for Grilled Pineapple Chutney.

2. Mix oil into remaining spice mixture; thoroughly baste fish.

3. Place fish on well-greased grill. Cook, covered, over medium-high direct heat for 10 to 15 minutes until opaque in center, turning once. Serve with Grilled Pineapple Chutney.

Makes 4 servings

Prep Time: 20 minutes • Cook Time: 15 minutes

Grilled Pineapple Chutney

½ of a fresh pineapple, peeled and sliced ½-inch thick
1 red or orange bell pepper, cut into quarters
2 tablespoons minced red onion
1 tablespoon minced candied ginger
1 tablespoon minced cilantro leaves

Grill pineapple and bell pepper about 10 minutes over medium direct heat until lightly charred and tender. Coarsely chop and place in bowl. Add reserved 3 tablespoons hot sauce mixture, onion, ginger and cilantro. Toss to combine.

Makes 3 cups

Grilled Red Snapper with Avocado-Papaya Salsa

  1 teaspoon ground coriander
  1 teaspoon paprika
  ¾ teaspoon salt
  ⅛ to ¼ teaspoon ground red pepper
  ½ cup diced ripe avocado
  ½ cup diced ripe papaya
  2 tablespoons chopped fresh cilantro
  1 tablespoon fresh lime juice
  1 tablespoon olive oil
  4 skinless red snapper or halibut fish fillets (5 to 7 ounces each)
  4 lime wedges

1. Combine coriander, paprika, salt and red pepper in small bowl; mix well.

2. Combine avocado, papaya, cilantro, lime juice and ¼ teaspoon spice mixture in medium bowl; mix well.

3. Oil grid. Prepare grill for direct cooking. Brush fish with olive oil. Sprinkle with remaining spice mixture. Grill fish over medium-high heat 10 minutes or until center is opaque, turning once.

4. Serve fish with salsa. Garnish with lime wedges.   *Makes 4 servings*

 TIP Snapper and halibut are relatively mild flavored fish, firm but more delicate than larger fish. When grilling seafood, turn over only once with a large two prong kitchen fork. Carefully insert it between the grill bars to slightly lift the fish. Then slide a metal spatula under the fish and turn.

Asian Honey-Tea Grilled Prawns

1½ pounds medium raw shrimp, peeled and deveined
    Salt
  2 green onions, thinly sliced

MARINADE
  1 cup brewed double-strength orange-spice tea, cooled
  ¼ cup honey
  ¼ cup rice vinegar
  ¼ cup soy sauce
  1 tablespoon finely chopped fresh ginger
  ½ teaspoon ground black pepper

In plastic food storage bag, combine marinade ingredients. Remove ½ cup marinade; set aside for dipping sauce. Add shrimp to marinade in bag, turning to coat. Close bag securely and marinate in refrigerator 30 minutes or up to 12 hours.

Remove shrimp from marinade; discard marinade. Thread shrimp onto 8 skewers, dividing evenly. Grill over medium coals 4 to 6 minutes or until shrimp turn pink and are just firm to the touch, turning once. Season with salt, as desired.

Meanwhile prepare dipping sauce by placing reserved ½ cup marinade in small saucepan. Bring to a boil over medium-high heat. Boil 3 to 5 minutes or until slightly reduced. Stir in green onions.

Makes 4 servings

Favorite recipe from **National Honey Board**

Grilled Chinese Salmon

3 tablespoons soy sauce
2 tablespoons dry sherry
2 cloves garlic, minced
4 salmon fillets (about 1 pound)
2 tablespoons finely chopped fresh cilantro

1. Combine soy sauce, sherry and garlic in shallow dish. Add salmon; turn to coat. Cover; refrigerate at least 30 minutes or up to 2 hours.

2. Oil grid. Prepare grill for direct cooking.

3. Remove salmon from dish; reserve marinade. Grill salmon, skin side down, over high heat 10 minutes or until center is opaque. Baste with reserved marinade after 5 minutes of grilling; discard any remaining marinade. Sprinkle with cilantro.   *Makes 4 servings*

Grilled Citrus Halibut

¼ cup lemon juice
3 tablespoons lime juice
3 tablespoons honey Dijon mustard
3 tablespoons olive oil
2 tablespoons MRS. DASH® Original Seasoning Blend
2 teaspoons MOLLY MC BUTTER® Natural Butter Flavor Sprinkles
1 pound halibut, cut into 4-ounce pieces

Combine all ingredients except halibut in resealable plastic bag, mixing well. Add halibut and seal bag. Marinate in refrigerator 30 to 60 minutes.

Remove halibut from bag and discard marinade.

Grill fish at medium high heat, 4 to 5 minutes per side, or until fish flakes easily.

Makes 4 servings

Prep Time: 10 minutes • Cook Time: 10 minutes

Grilled Chinese Salmon

Grilled Baja Burritos

1 pound tilapia fillets
4 tablespoons vegetable oil, divided
3 tablespoons lime juice, divided
2 teaspoons chili powder
1½ teaspoons lemon pepper
3 cups coleslaw mix
½ cup chopped cilantro
¼ teaspoon salt
¼ teaspoon black pepper
Guacamole and pico de gallo
4 (7-inch) flour tortillas
Lime wedges

1. Place tilapia, 2 tablespoons oil, 1 tablespoon lime juice, chili powder and lemon pepper in large resealable food storage bag. Seal bag; turn to coat. Let stand 10 minutes.

2. Combine coleslaw mix, cilantro, remaining 2 tablespoons oil, salt and black pepper in medium bowl; set aside.

3. Oil grid. Prepare grill for direct cooking. Grill fish over medium-high heat 6 to 8 minutes or until center is opaque.

4. Layer fish, coleslaw mixture, guacamole and pico de gallo on bottom of tortillas. Tightly roll up bottom and sides of tortilla. Serve with lime wedges.

Makes 4 servings

 TIP Any firm white fish, such as snapper or halibut, can be substituted for the tilapia. For delicate fish like tilapia, a grill topper or basket helps prevent the fish from breaking apart on the grid.

Grilled Scallop Salad with Hot Bacon Vinaigrette

4 strips bacon, chopped
½ cup prepared Italian or vinaigrette salad dressing
⅓ cup *French's®* Honey Dijon Mustard or *French's®* Honey Mustard
2 tablespoons water
8 cups mixed salad greens
1 cup diced yellow bell peppers
1 cup halved cherry tomatoes
½ cup pine nuts
1 pound sea scallops

1. Cook bacon until crisp in medium skillet. Whisk in salad dressing, mustard and water; keep warm over very low heat.

2. Place salad greens, bell pepper, tomatoes and nuts in large bowl; toss. Arrange on salad plates; set aside.

3. Season scallops with salt and pepper to taste. Cook in an electric grill pan or barbecue grill 3 minutes until just opaque in centers. Arrange scallops on salad plates, dividing evenly. Serve with dressing. *Makes 4 servings*

Prep Time: 10 minutes • Cook Time: 5 minutes

 TIP Butterflied shrimp are a good substitute for scallops, or grill both for a mixed seafood salad. To butterfly shrimp, split the shrimp down the center of the back with a sharp knife, cutting almost through to make them lie flat. Scallops and shrimp both cook very quickly on the grill. Brush lightly with additional oil or dressing to keep them moist.

Lemon Herbed Seafood Kabobs

  2 tablespoons vegetable oil
  2 tablespoons finely chopped onion
  ¼ teaspoon dried rosemary
  ¼ teaspoon dried thyme leaves
  ½ SUNKIST® lemon, grated zest
  1 SUNKIST® lemon, juiced
  ¼ teaspoon salt
  1 pound halibut or shark steak, cut into 1-inch cubes *or*
      1 pound sea scallops (16 to 20)
 12 pieces (1 inch square) red or green bell pepper
 12 medium button mushrooms

•In small nonstick skillet, heat oil; add onion, rosemary, thyme and lemon zest. Cook over low heat 1 to 2 minutes to infuse oil. Remove from heat; add lemon juice and salt. Cool. Pour oil mixture over fish in resealable plastic food storage bag. Seal bag and marinate in refrigerator 1 hour or longer, turning occasionally.

•To make kabobs, arrange drained fish, bell pepper and mushrooms alternately on four 10-inch metal skewers. Lightly brush mushrooms, peppers and fish with small amount of additional oil.

•Barbecue on grill 4 to 6 inches above glowing coals, on medium heat of gas barbecue or broil 4 inches from heat 12 to 14 minutes or until fish is opaque and flakes easily with fork (turning about 3 times). *Makes 4 servings*

 TIP Wooden skewers, soaked in water 30 minutes, are ideal for kabobs. Using the double skewer technique makes the ingredients more stable and easier to turn. Just thread the pieces onto one skewer, then run another through the pieces parallel to the first. Since the food will not rotate when turning, everything will be evenly cooked.

Blackened Catfish with Creole Vegetables

⅔ cup *Cattlemen's®* Authentic Smoke House Barbecue Sauce or *Cattlemen's* Award
    Winning Classic Barbecue Sauce
⅓ cup *Frank's® RedHot® Chile 'n Lime*™ Hot Sauce or *Frank's® RedHot®* Cayenne
    Pepper Sauce
2 tablespoons Southwest chile seasoning blend or Cajun blend seasoning
1 tablespoon olive oil
4 skinless catfish or sea bass fillets (1½ pounds)
    Salt and pepper to taste
    Creole Vegetables (recipe follows)

1. Combine barbecue sauce, *Chile 'n Lime*™ Hot Sauce, seasoning blend and oil. Reserve ½ cup mixture for Creole Vegetables.

2. Season fish with salt and pepper to taste. Baste fish with remaining barbecue sauce mixture.

3. Cook fish on a well-greased grill over medium direct heat 5 minutes per side until fish is opaque in center, turning once. Serve with Creole Vegetables. *Makes 4 servings*

Prep Time: 20 minutes • Cook Time: 15 minutes

Creole Vegetables

1 red, green or orange bell pepper, cut into pieces
1 large green zucchini or summer squash, cut in half crosswise, then lengthwise
    into thick slices
1 large white onion, sliced ½-inch thick
    Vegetable cooking spray

Arrange vegetables on skewers. Coat vegetables with cooking spray. Grill vegetables over medium direct heat until lightly charred and tender, basting often with reserved ½ cup barbecue sauce mixture. *Makes 4 servings*

Grilled Sea Bass with Ripe Olive 'n' Caper Salsa

  1 cup sliced California Ripe Olives
½ cup seeded, diced Roma tomatoes
½ cup chopped oil-packed sun-dried tomatoes
¼ cup minced red onion
¼ cup chopped fresh basil
  3 tablespoons capers
  2 tablespoons chopped fresh parsley
  2 tablespoons balsamic-style vinaigrette dressing
  1 teaspoon minced garlic
  8 (6-ounce) sea bass or other white fish fillets
    Olive oil

Preheat grill or broiler. For Ripe Olive 'n' Caper Salsa, combine all ingredients except sea bass and olive oil in large bowl. Mix well. Adjust seasoning with salt and pepper. Cover and chill. Brush both sides of fillets with olive oil and season with salt and pepper. Grill or broil until fish is firm to the touch, about 5 minutes on each side. Serve each fillet with about ¼ cup of Ripe Olive 'n' Caper Salsa.

Makes 8 servings

Favorite recipe from **California Olive Industry**

Honey BBQ Bourbon Salmon

¾ cup *Cattlemen's*® Golden Honey Barbecue Sauce
  3 tablespoons bourbon
  4 salmon fillets, 4×2×1 inches
    Salt and black pepper to taste

1. Combine barbecue sauce and bourbon; set aside.

2. Season salmon with salt and pepper to taste. Generously baste barbecue sauce mixture on both sides of salmon pieces.

3. Cook salmon on a well-greased grill over medium heat for 12 to 15 minutes until opaque in center, turning and basting once. Serve with additional barbecue sauce. *Makes 4 servings*

Note: If desired, bourbon may be omitted or substituted with orange juice.

Prep Time: 5 minutes • Cook Time: 12 minutes

Grilled Sea Bass with Ripe Olive
'n' Caper Salsa

Asian Shrimp & Steak Kabobs

1 envelope LIPTON® RECIPE SECRETS® Savory Herb with Garlic or Onion Soup Mix
¼ cup soy sauce
¼ cup lemon juice
¼ cup BERTOLLI® Olive Oil
¼ cup honey
½ pound uncooked medium shrimp, peeled and deveined
½ pound boneless sirloin steak, cut into 1-inch cubes
16 cherry tomatoes
2 cups mushroom caps
1 medium green bell pepper, cut into chunks

1. In 13×9-inch glass baking dish, blend soup mix, soy sauce, lemon juice, olive oil and honey; set aside.

2. On skewers, alternately thread shrimp, steak, tomatoes, mushrooms and green pepper. Add prepared skewers to baking dish; turn to coat. Cover and marinate in refrigerator, turning skewers occasionally, at least 2 hours. Remove prepared skewers from marinade; reserve marinade.

3. Grill or broil, turning and basting frequently with reserved marinade, until shrimp turn pink and steak is cooked to desired doneness. Do not brush with marinade during last 5 minutes of cooking.

Makes 4 servings

Salmon with Warm Mango Salsa

1 salmon fillet, about 1 inch thick (1¼ pounds)
4 sheets (18×12 inches) heavy-duty foil, lightly sprayed with nonstick cooking spray
½ teaspoon paprika
⅛ teaspoon ground red pepper
2 medium mangoes, peeled, seeded and cut into ¾-inch pieces
½ medium red bell pepper, chopped
1 jalapeño pepper,* seeded and finely chopped
2 tablespoons chopped fresh parsley
1 tablespoon thawed frozen orange-pineapple juice concentrate or orange juice concentrate

*Jalapeño peppers can sting and irritate the skin, so wear rubber gloves when handling peppers and do not touch your eyes.

1. Prepare grill for direct cooking.

2. Pat salmon dry with paper towels. Cut into 4 pieces. Place one piece of salmon, skin side down, on each sheet of foil. Combine paprika and red pepper in small bowl. Rub on tops of salmon pieces.

3. Combine mangoes, bell pepper, jalapeño, parsley and juice concentrate in medium bowl. Spoon onto salmon pieces.

4. Double fold sides and ends of foil to seal packets, leaving head space for heat circulation. Place on baking sheet.

5. Grill packets, covered, over medium-high heat 10 minutes or until center of fish is opaque. Carefully open one end of each packet to allow steam to escape. Open packets and transfer contents to serving plates.

Makes 4 servings

Surf & Turf Kabobs

1 pound beef tenderloin, cut into 1¼-inch pieces

12 jumbo raw shrimp, peeled and deveined, tails intact

1 medium onion, cut into 12 wedges

1 red or yellow bell pepper, cut into 1-inch chunks

⅓ cup butter, melted

3 tablespoons lemon juice

3 cloves garlic, minced

2 teaspoons paprika or smoked paprika

1 teaspoon salt

¼ teaspoon black pepper or ground red pepper

Lemon wedges

1. Alternately thread beef, shrimp, onion and bell pepper onto 12-inch metal skewers. (Skewer shrimp through ends to form "C" shape for even cooking.)

2. Combine butter, lemon juice, garlic, paprika, salt and black pepper in small bowl.

3. Prepare grill for direct cooking. Place skewers on grid over medium heat; brush with half of butter mixture. Grill 5 minutes; turn and brush with remaining butter sauce. Continue grilling 5 to 6 minutes or until shrimp are opaque (beef will be medium-rare to medium doneness). Serve with lemon wedges.

Makes 4 servings

 TIP Be sure to purchase jumbo shrimp for this recipe. The shrimp and steak should be approximately the same size so they will cook evenly.

Grilled Swordfish Sicilian Style

  3 tablespoons extra virgin olive oil
  1 clove garlic, minced
  2 tablespoons lemon juice
  ¾ teaspoon salt
  ⅛ teaspoon black pepper
  3 tablespoons capers, drained
  1 tablespoon chopped fresh oregano or basil
1½ pounds swordfish steaks (¾ inch thick)

1. Oil grid. Prepare grill for direct cooking.

2. For sauce, heat oil in small saucepan over low heat; add garlic. Cook 1 minute. Remove from heat; cool slightly. Whisk in lemon juice, salt and pepper until salt is dissolved. Stir in capers and oregano.

3. Grill swordfish over medium heat 14 to 16 minutes or until center is opaque, turning once. Serve fish with sauce.

Makes 4 to 6 servings

TIP Swordfish is popular for its mild flavor and meaty texture. Be sure to grill on an oiled grid or lightly drizzle both sides with oil before cooking to keep it from sticking to the grid. With its firm texture, swordfish is also a good choice for fish kabobs.

Grilled Lobster, Shrimp and Calamari Ceviche

¾ cup orange juice
⅓ cup fresh lime juice
  2 jalapeño peppers,* seeded and minced
  2 tablespoons chopped fresh cilantro, chives or green onion tops
  2 tablespoons tequila
  1 teaspoon honey
  1 teaspoon ground cumin
  1 teaspoon olive oil
  1 quart water
10 squid, cleaned and cut into rings and tentacles
½ pound medium raw shrimp, peeled and deveined
  2 lobster tails (8 ounces each), meat removed and shells discarded

*Jalapeño peppers can sting and irritate the skin, so wear rubber gloves when handling peppers and do not touch your eyes.

1. For marinade, combine orange juice, lime juice, jalapeños, cilantro, tequila and honey in medium bowl. Remove ¼ cup marinade to small bowl; stir in cumin and oil. Set aside. Refrigerate remaining marinade.

2. Bring water to a boil in large saucepan over high heat. Add squid; cook 30 seconds or until opaque. Rinse under cold water; drain. Add squid to refrigerated marinade.

3. Prepare grill for direct cooking. Thread shrimp onto metal skewers. Brush shrimp and lobster with reserved ¼ cup marinade.

4. Grill shrimp, uncovered, over medium-high heat 2 to 3 minutes per side or until pink and opaque. Remove shrimp from skewers; add to squid. Grill lobster 5 minutes per side or until meat is opaque and cooked through. Slice lobster meat into ¼-inch-thick slices; add to squid and shrimp mixture.

5. Refrigerate at least 2 hours or overnight.

Makes 6 appetizer servings

Garlic Skewered Shrimp

1 pound large raw shrimp, peeled and deveined
2 tablespoons soy sauce
1 tablespoon vegetable oil
3 cloves garlic, minced
¼ teaspoon red pepper flakes (optional)
3 green onions, cut into 1-inch pieces

1. Soak four 12-inch wooden skewers in water 30 minutes. Meanwhile, place shrimp in large resealable food storage bag. Combine soy sauce, oil, garlic and red pepper flakes, if desired, in small bowl; mix well. Pour over shrimp. Seal bag; turn to coat. Marinate at room temperature about 15 minutes.

2. Prepare grill for direct cooking. Remove shrimp from marinade; reserve marinade. Alternately thread shrimp and onions onto skewers. Brush with reserved marinade; discard any remaining marinade. Grill, covered, 5 minutes per side or until shrimp are pink and opaque.

Makes 4 servings

 **SERVING SUGGESTION** For a more attractive presentation, leave the tails on the shrimp.

Barbecue
Sidekicks

Chili-Rubbed Grilled Vegetable Kabobs

2 ears corn on the cob, husked and cleaned
1 medium sweet or red onion, cut through core into 12 wedges
1 red bell pepper, cut into 12 (1-inch) chunks
1 yellow bell pepper, cut into 12 (1-inch) chunks
1 green bell pepper, cut into 12 (1-inch) chunks
2 tablespoons olive oil
1 teaspoon seasoned salt
1 teaspoon chili powder
½ teaspoon sugar

1. Cut cobs crosswise into 1-inch pieces with large chef's knife. Alternately thread corn, onion and bell peppers onto 12-inch metal skewers. Brush oil evenly over vegetables. Combine seasoned salt, chili powder and sugar; sprinkle on all sides of vegetables. Wrap skewers in heavy-duty foil; refrigerate up to 8 hours.

2. Prepare grill for direct cooking. Unwrap skewers; place on grid over medium heat. Grill 10 to 12 minutes or until vegetables are tender, turning occasionally. *Makes 4 servings*

Easy Summer Vegetable Medley

2 medium red or green bell peppers, cut into chunks
2 medium zucchini or summer squash, sliced lengthwise in half and
   then into thick slices
1 (12-ounce) package mushrooms, cleaned and cut into quarters
3 carrots, thinly sliced
1⅓ cups *French's®* French Fried Onions or *French's®* Cheddar French Fried Onions
¼ cup fresh basil, minced
2 tablespoons olive oil
   Salt and black pepper to taste
2 ice cubes
1 large foil oven roasting bag

1. Toss all ingredients in large bowl. Open foil bag; spoon mixture into bag in even layer. Seal bag with tight double folds. Place bag on baking sheet.

2. Place bag on grill over medium-high heat. Cover grill and cook 15 minutes until vegetables are tender, turning bag over once.

3. Return bag to baking sheet and carefully cut top of bag open. Sprinkle with additional French Fried Onions, if desired.   *Makes 4 to 6 servings*

Prep Time: 10 minutes • Cook Time: 15 minutes

 TIP Foil bags work great for cooking vegetables along with other food on the grill. They are also very helpful to transport vegetables to a cookout. When cooking over a campfire, put the bag directly on medium-low coals, turning frequently to prevent the contents from burning. Be sure to open the bag carefully to avoid getting burned by hot escaping steam.

Grilled Asparagus and Peppers

½ cup balsamic vinegar
¼ cup olive oil
 1 tablespoon chopped onion
 1 clove garlic, minced
½ teaspoon dried basil
½ teaspoon dried thyme
½ teaspoon lemon pepper
¼ teaspoon salt
 1 pound thin asparagus, trimmed
 1 large red bell pepper, cut into ½-inch-wide strips
 1 large yellow bell pepper, cut into ½-inch-wide strips

1. Combine vinegar, oil, onion, garlic, basil, thyme, lemon pepper and salt in small bowl until blended. Place vinegar mixture, asparagus and bell peppers in large resealable food storage bag. Seal bag; turn to coat. Marinate 30 minutes, turning once.

2. Prepare grill for direct cooking.

3. Remove asparagus and bell peppers from marinade; reserve marinade. Grill over medium-high heat 8 to 10 minutes or until tender, turning halfway through grilling time and brushing frequently with reserved marinade.

Makes 5 to 6 servings

 TIP Nothing is easier than grilling asparagus. Remove any woody stems, brush with marinade or olive oil and place on the grid. Cook for about 5 minutes, watching carefully and turning occasionally. Grill extra asparagus—and bell peppers—to use in salads later in the week.

Sesame Portobello Mushrooms

4 large portobello mushrooms
2 tablespoons sweet rice wine
2 tablespoons soy sauce
2 cloves garlic, minced
1 teaspoon dark sesame oil

1. Prepare grill for direct cooking.

2. Remove and discard stems from mushrooms; set caps aside. Combine wine, soy sauce, garlic and oil in small bowl.

3. Brush both sides of mushroom caps with soy sauce mixture. Grill mushrooms, top sides up, covered, over medium heat 3 to 4 minutes. Brush tops with soy sauce mixture; turn. Grill 2 minutes more or until mushrooms are lightly browned. Turn again; grill, basting frequently, 4 to 5 minutes or until tender when pressed with back of metal spatula. Cut diagonally into ½-inch-thick slices.

Makes 4 servings

 TIP Portobello mushrooms—a great choice for vegetarian meals—are very easy and delicious on the grill. Their meaty texture and intense flavor stand up to bold marinades. Large portobellos are also perfect to serve in a sandwich bun as a burger.

Grilled Beet Salad

6 medium red beets (about 1½ pounds), peeled
1 medium yellow onion, cut into ½-inch wedges
½ pound carrots, halved lengthwise and cut into 1-inch pieces
¼ cup plus 2 tablespoons olive oil, divided
3 to 4 tablespoons balsamic vinegar
1 clove garlic, minced
½ teaspoon salt
½ teaspoon dried rosemary
¼ teaspoon black pepper
6 cups chopped spring greens *or* 2 packages (5 ounces each) spring mix
2 ounces Gorgonzola or goat cheese, crumbled
1 cup pecan pieces, toasted,* or candied pecans

*To toast pecans, spread in single layer in heavy skillet. Cook over medium heat 1 to 2 minutes or until lightly browned, stirring frequently.

1. Prepare grill for direct cooking.

2. Cut beets into 1-inch pieces; place in microwavable dish. Cover; microwave on HIGH 6 to 8 minutes or until slightly soft. Cool to room temperature.

3. Place beets, onions and carrots in single layer in two 12×8 disposable foil pans. Drizzle vegetables in each pan with 1 tablespoon oil; stir to coat. Cover loosely with foil. Grill over medium-high heat 22 to 25 minutes until fork-tender, stirring frequently. Cool completely.

4. For vinaigrette, combine remaining ¼ cup oil, vinegar, garlic, salt, rosemary and pepper in small bowl; mix well.

5. Place greens in salad bowl. Add half of vinaigrette; toss gently. Top with grilled vegetables; drizzle with remaining vinaigrette. Sprinkle with cheese and pecans. Serve immediately.

Makes 4 servings

Note: To peel beets, trim ends, then peel with a vegetable peeler under running water to help minimize the beet juice from staining your hands.

Grilled Vegetable Pizzas

2 tablespoons olive oil
1 clove garlic, minced
1 red bell pepper, cut into quarters
4 slices red onion, cut ¼ inch thick
1 medium zucchini, halved lengthwise
1 medium yellow squash, halved lengthwise
1 cup prepared pizza sauce
¼ teaspoon red pepper flakes
2 (10-inch) prepared pizza crusts
2 cups (8 ounces) shredded fontinella or mozzarella cheese
¼ cup sliced fresh basil leaves

1. Prepare grill for direct cooking.

2. Combine oil and garlic in small bowl; brush over bell pepper, onion, zucchini and squash. Grill vegetables, covered, over medium heat 10 minutes or until crisp-tender, turning halfway through grilling time.

3. Slice bell pepper lengthwise into ¼-inch strips. Cut zucchini and squash crosswise into ¼-inch slices. Separate onion slices into rings.

4. Combine pizza sauce and red pepper flakes in small bowl. Top crusts with pizza sauce mixture, cheese and grilled vegetables.

5. Grill pizzas, covered, over medium-low heat. Grill, covered, 5 to 6 minutes or until cheese is melted and crusts are hot. Sprinkle pizzas with basil; cut into wedges.   *Makes 4 to 6 servings*

Grilled Potato Salad

¼ cup country-style Dijon mustard
2 tablespoons chopped fresh dill
1 tablespoon white wine or apple cider vinegar
1½ teaspoons salt, divided
¼ teaspoon black pepper
5 tablespoons olive oil, divided
8 cups water
2 pounds small red potatoes, cut into ½-inch slices
1 green onion, thinly sliced

1. Whisk mustard, dill, vinegar, ½ teaspoon salt and pepper in small bowl. Gradually whisk in 3 tablespoons oil. Set aside.

2. Bring water and remaining 1 teaspoon salt to a boil in large saucepan over medium-high heat. Add potatoes; boil about 5 minutes. Drain; return to saucepan. Drizzle with remaining 2 tablespoons olive oil; toss lightly.

3. Prepare grill for direct cooking. Spray large sheet of foil with nonstick cooking spray. Transfer potatoes to foil; fold into packet. Grill packet over medium-high heat 7 to 10 minutes or until potatoes are tender. Transfer potatoes to serving bowl. Sprinkle with green onion. Toss gently with dressing. Serve warm.

Makes 4 servings

Jamaican Grilled Sweet Potatoes

2 large sweet potatoes or yams (about 1½ pounds)
3 tablespoons packed brown sugar
3 tablespoons melted butter, divided
1 teaspoon ground ginger
1 tablespoon chopped fresh cilantro
2 teaspoons dark rum

1. Pierce potatoes in several places with fork; place on paper towels. Microwave on HIGH 5 to 6 minutes or until crisp-tender. Let stand 10 minutes. Diagonally slice potatoes into ¾-inch slices.

2. Combine brown sugar, 1 tablespoon butter and ginger in small bowl; mix well. Stir in cilantro and rum; set aside.

3. Lightly brush one side of sweet potato slices with 1 tablespoon butter. Grill sweet potatoes, buttered side down, covered, over medium heat 4 to 6 minutes or until grill marks appear. Brush tops with remaining 1 tablespoon butter. Turn; grill 3 to 5 minutes or until tender. Serve with rum butter.

Makes 6 servings

BBQ Corn Wheels

4 ears corn on the cob, husked and cleaned
3 red, green or yellow bell peppers, cut into large chunks
¾ cup barbecue sauce
½ cup honey
¼ cup *French's®* Worcestershire Sauce
Vegetable cooking spray

1. Cut corn into 1-inch slices. Alternately thread corn and pepper chunks onto four metal skewers. (Pierce tip of skewer through center of corn wheel to thread.) Combine barbecue sauce, honey and Worcestershire.

2. Coat kabobs with vegetable cooking spray. Grill kabobs on greased rack over medium heat for 5 minutes. Cook 5 minutes more until corn is tender, turning and basting with barbecue sauce mixture. Serve any extra sauce on the side with grilled hamburgers, steaks or chicken.

Makes 4 servings

Prep Time: 10 minutes • Cook Time: 10 minutes

Jamaican Grilled
Sweet Potatoes

Herb Grilled Vegetables

¾ cup olive oil
¼ cup red wine vinegar
2 to 3 tablespoons finely chopped mixed fresh herbs *or* 2 teaspoons mixed
    dried herbs
1 tablespoon lemon pepper
2 cloves garlic, minced
1 medium eggplant (about 1¼ pounds)
2 medium zucchini
2 to 3 medium yellow squash
2 medium red bell peppers

1. Whisk oil, vinegar, herbs, lemon pepper and garlic in small bowl.

2. Slice eggplant, zucchini and yellow squash lengthwise into ½-inch slices. Cut bell peppers into 1-inch strips. Place vegetables in 13×9-inch baking dish. Pour oil mixture over vegetables; turn to coat. Marinate 30 minutes.

3. Prepare grill for direct cooking.

4. Remove vegetables from marinade; reserve marinade in dish. Grill, covered, over medium heat 8 to 16 minutes or until fork-tender, turning once or twice.

5. Return grilled vegetables to baking dish; turn to coat with remaining marinade. Serve warm or at room temperature.

Makes 6 servings

 TIP Grilling eggplant concentrates the flavor and transforms the texture into a tender, creamy consistency. For large eggplants, peel and cut crosswise into rounds. For small eggplants, cut lengthwise into long thin slices. Make sure to cut the pieces the same thickness to ensure even cooking.

Grilled Vegetable Escalivada

VINAIGRETTE

⅓ cup sherry wine vinegar

⅓ cup balsamic vinegar

⅓ cup olive oil

½ teaspoon salt

½ teaspoon ground black pepper

VEGETABLES

2 medium onions, cut into thick wedges

6 thin asparagus spears

6 yellow summer squash, halved lengthwise

1 eggplant, cut into thick slices

1 red bell pepper, cut into 6 wedges

1 green bell pepper, cut into 6 wedges

1 yellow bell pepper, cut into 6 wedges

FOR VINAIGRETTE DRESSING

Whisk together all ingredients.*

FOR VEGETABLES

Brush vegetables with olive oil and grill 4 to 6 inches over medium coals for 10 to 20 minutes, turning once, until vegetables are tender and slightly charred. Place vegetables on serving platter and drizzle with vinaigrette dressing.   *Makes 4 to 6 servings*

*Makes about 1 cup.

Favorite recipe from **National Onion Association**

Grilled Sweet Potato Packets with Pecan Butter

4 sweet potatoes (about 8 ounces each), peeled and cut into ¼-inch slices
1 large sweet or Spanish onion, thinly sliced and separated into rings
3 tablespoons vegetable oil
⅓ cup butter, softened
2 tablespoons packed brown sugar
¼ teaspoon salt
¼ teaspoon ground cinnamon
¼ cup chopped pecans

1. Prepare grill for direct cooking.

2. Alternately place potato slices and onion rings on four 14×12-inch sheets of heavy-duty foil. Brush with oil. Double fold sides and ends of foil to seal packets.

3. Grill packets, covered, over medium heat 25 to 30 minutes or until potatoes are fork-tender.

4. Meanwhile, combine butter, brown sugar, salt and cinnamon in small bowl; mix well. Stir in pecans. Serve with sweet potatoes. *Makes 4 servings*

 TIP Starchy vegetables such as potatoes and carrots should be partially cooked before grilling over direct heat. Either steam or cook 2 to 3 minutes in the microwave before finishing on the grill. Par-cooking is not needed when cooking starchy vegetables in a foil packet.

Grilled Vegetables with Creamy Polenta

1 head garlic, separated into cloves
½ pound plum tomatoes
1 green bell pepper, quartered
1 red or orange bell pepper, quartered
2 medium zucchini
2 ears corn
3 tablespoons prepared pesto
4½ cups water
½ teaspoon salt
⅛ teaspoon black pepper
1 cup polenta or yellow cornmeal
⅓ cup shredded Parmesan cheese
2 teaspoons butter

1. Prepare grill for direct cooking.

2. Place garlic on 10-inch piece of foil; lightly spray with nonstick cooking spray. Double fold sides and ends of foil to seal packets. Grill packets over medium-low heat about 20 minutes or until tender, turning frequently. Cool; peel garlic.

3. Cut tomatoes in half lengthwise; remove seeds. Grill tomatoes and peppers, skin side down, over high heat until blackened. Place bell peppers in paper bag; let stand 5 minutes. Remove skin from tomatoes and bell peppers. Cut into bite-size pieces; place in large bowl.

4. Cut zucchini lengthwise into ¼-inch slices; spray lightly with cooking spray. Grill zucchini and corn over medium heat 2 to 6 minutes or until tender and lightly browned, turning once. Cut zucchini into small pieces; cut corn off cob. Add to bowl. Add garlic and pesto; toss to coat. Keep warm.

5. Bring water to a boil in medium saucepan; add salt and black pepper. Slowly stir in polenta; cook and stir over medium heat about 5 minutes or until creamy and thickened. Stir in cheese and butter; add additional water as needed to keep creamy consistency.

6. Spoon vegetables over polenta; serve immediately.

Makes 4 servings

Grilled Tri-Colored Pepper Salad

1 *each* large red, yellow and green bell pepper, cut into halves or quarters
⅓ cup extra virgin olive oil
3 tablespoons balsamic vinegar
2 cloves garlic, minced
¼ teaspoon salt
¼ teaspoon black pepper
⅓ cup crumbled goat cheese (about 1½ ounces)
¼ cup thinly sliced fresh basil

1. Prepare grill for direct cooking.

2. Grill bell peppers, skin side down, covered, over high heat 10 to 12 minutes or until skin is charred. Place charred bell peppers in paper bag. Close bag; set aside to cool 5 to 10 minutes. Remove skin; discard.

3. Place bell peppers in shallow glass serving dish. Combine oil, vinegar, garlic, salt and black pepper in small bowl; whisk until well combined. Pour over bell peppers. Let stand 30 minutes at room temperature. (Or cover and refrigerate up to 24 hours. Bring bell peppers to room temperature before serving.)

4. Sprinkle bell peppers with cheese and basil just before serving.   *Makes 4 to 6 servings*

 TIP You can't beat the flavor and versatility of grilled bell peppers. This delicious grilled pepper salad can be prepared early and held until ready to serve. Grill extra peppers for salad toppings and sandwich fillings later in the week.

Grilled Veggies and Couscous

⅓ cup pine nuts
1½ cups vegetable broth or water
2 tablespoons olive oil, divided
½ teaspoon salt
1 cup uncooked couscous
1 medium zucchini, cut lengthwise into ½-inch slices
½ small red onion, cut into 5 (½-inch) slices
1 medium red bell pepper, cut in half
¼ cup crumbled plain or tomato basil-flavored feta cheese
1 clove garlic, minced
½ teaspoon lemon pepper
Salt and black pepper

1. Spread pine nuts in small nonstick skillet; cook over low heat about 5 minutes or until light brown and fragrant. Set aside to cool.

2. Bring broth, 1 tablespoon oil and salt to a boil in small saucepan over medium heat. Stir in couscous. Cover; remove from heat. Set aside.

3. Prepare grill for direct cooking. Brush vegetables with remaining 1 tablespoon oil. Grill zucchini and onion over medium-high heat 3 to 5 minutes or until tender. Grill bell pepper 7 to 10 minutes or until blackened. Place pepper in paper bag; set aside 5 minutes. Remove from bag; peel off blackened skin. Dice vegetables.

4. Spoon couscous into serving bowl. Fluff with fork. Add diced vegetables, pine nuts, cheese, garlic and lemon pepper. Season with salt and black pepper.

Makes 6 servings

Buffalo Chili Onions

½ cup *Frank's® RedHot®* Original Cayenne Pepper Sauce
½ cup (1 stick) butter or margarine, melted or olive oil
¼ cup Cattleman's® Award Winning Classic Barbecue Sauce
1 tablespoon chili powder
4 large sweet onions, cut into ½-inch-thick slices

1. Whisk together *Frank's® RedHot®* Sauce, butter, barbecue sauce and chili powder in medium bowl until blended; brush on onion slices.

2. Place onions on grid. Grill over medium-high heat 10 minutes or until tender, turning and basting often with the chili mixture. Serve warm. *Makes 6 side-dish servings*

Tip: Onions may be prepared ahead and grilled just before serving.

Variation: To make Grilled Buffalo Garlic Bread, combine ¼ cup each *Frank's® RedHot®* Sauce and melted butter with 1 teaspoon minced garlic. Lightly brush on thick slices of Italian bread. Grill or toast until golden. Top with blue cheese crumbles, if desired.

Prep Time: **10 minutes** • Cook Time: **10 minutes**

Grilled Cajun Potato Wedges

3 large unpeeled russet potatoes, washed and scrubbed (about 2¼ pounds)
¼ cup olive oil
2 cloves garlic, minced
1 teaspoon salt
1 teaspoon paprika
½ teaspoon dried thyme leaves
½ teaspoon dried oregano leaves
¼ teaspoon black pepper
⅛ to ¼ teaspoon ground red pepper
2 cups mesquite chips

1. Preheat oven to 425°F.

2. Cut potatoes in half lengthwise; then cut each half lengthwise into four wedges. Place potatoes in large bowl. Add oil and garlic; toss to coat.

3. Combine salt, paprika, thyme, oregano, black pepper and red pepper in small bowl. Sprinkle over potatoes; toss to coat. Place potato wedges in single layer in shallow roasting pan; reserve remaining oil mixture left in large bowl. Bake 20 minutes.

4. Meanwhile, cover mesquite chips with cold water; soak 20 minutes. Prepare grill for direct cooking. Drain mesquite chips; sprinkle over coals. Grill potato wedges, cut sides down, covered, over medium heat 15 to 20 minutes or until potatoes are browned and fork-tender, brushing with reserved oil mixture halfway through grilling time and turning once.   *Makes 4 to 6 servings*

Grilled Sesame Asparagus

1 pound medium asparagus spears (about 20), trimmed
1 tablespoon sesame seeds
2 to 3 teaspoons balsamic vinegar
¼ teaspoon salt
¼ teaspoon pepper

1. Oil grid. Prepare grill for direct cooking.

2. Place asparagus on baking sheet; spray lightly with nonstick cooking spray. Sprinkle with sesame seeds, rolling to coat.

3. Grill asparagus, uncovered, 4 to 6 minutes or until beginning to brown, turning once.

4. Transfer asparagus to serving dish. Sprinkle with vinegar, salt and pepper.

Makes 4 servings

Szechuan Grilled Mushrooms

1 pound large fresh mushrooms
2 tablespoons soy sauce
2 teaspoons peanut or vegetable oil
1 teaspoon dark sesame oil
1 clove garlic, minced
½ teaspoon crushed Szechuan peppercorns or red pepper flakes

1. Place mushrooms in large resealable food storage bag. Add soy sauce, peanut oil, sesame oil, garlic and peppercorns to bag. Seal bag; turn to coat. Marinate at room temperature 15 minutes.

2. Thread mushrooms onto skewers. Grill mushrooms 5 inches from heat 10 minutes or until lightly browned, turning once. Serve immediately. *Makes 4 servings*

Variation: Add 4 green onions, cut into 1½-inch pieces, to marinade. Alternately thread onto skewers with mushrooms. Proceed as directed in step 2.

Grilled Bok Choy Packets

12 fresh or dried shiitake mushrooms*
½ small onion, thinly sliced
 1 head bok choy (1 pound), coarsely chopped
 1 can (about 8¾ ounces) whole baby corn, rinsed and drained
 1 large red bell pepper, cut into strips
 2 tablespoons water
 2 tablespoons sweet rice wine
 2 tablespoons soy sauce
1½ teaspoons dark sesame oil
 1 teaspoon minced fresh ginger
½ teaspoon salt

*For dried mushrooms, place in small bowl; cover with warm water and soak 30 minutes to soften. Drain and squeeze dry.

1. Prepare grill for direct cooking. Remove and discard mushroom stems; set aside.

2. Spray six 16-inch-long sheets of foil with nonstick cooking spray. Layer onion slices, bok choy, corn, bell pepper and mushrooms in center of each sheet.

3. Combine water, rice wine, soy sauce, sesame oil, ginger and salt in small bowl. Drizzle over vegetables in each packet.

4. Double fold sides and ends of packets, leaving head space for heat circulation. Turn packets over several times to coat vegetables completely.

5. Grill packets, covered, over medium heat about 10 minutes, turning every 2 to 3 minutes. To serve, carefully open one end of each packet and slide vegetables onto plates.

Makes 6 servings

Mango-Banana Foster

2 medium mangoes, peeled, seeded and chopped

2 firm ripe bananas, cut into ¾-inch-thick slices

8 maraschino cherries, halved

½ cup packed brown sugar

2 tablespoons rum *or* 2 tablespoons orange juice plus ¼ teaspoon rum extract

½ teaspoon ground cinnamon

Vanilla ice cream

1. Prepare grill for direct cooking.

2. Place mangoes, bananas and cherries evenly in center of four 18×12-inch sheets of heavy-duty foil. Stir together brown sugar, rum and cinnamon in small bowl; spoon over fruit.

3. Double fold sides and ends of foil to seal packets, leaving head space for heat circulation.

4. Grill packets, covered, over medium-high heat 3 to 5 minutes or until hot. Carefully open one end of each packet to allow steam to escape.

5. Spoon ice cream into serving bowls. Open packets; pour fruit and sauce over ice cream.

Makes 4 servings

 TIP To easily transport foil packets to the grill, place prepared packets on a baking sheet. Then slide the packets off the baking sheet directly onto the grid.

Grilled Pineapple with Caramel Dipping Sauce

25 unwrapped caramels
⅓ cup half-and-half
¼ teaspoon rum extract
1 ripe pineapple, trimmed and sliced into 8 (½-inch) slices

1. Prepare grill for direct cooking.

2. Place caramels, half-and-half and rum extract in small saucepan. Cook and stir over medium-low heat until sauce is thick and smooth. Keep warm.

3. Grill pineapple over medium-high heat about 10 to 12 minutes or until pineapple softens and turns deeper yellow in color, turning once.

4. Cut pineapple into bite-size pieces, discarding core. Serve pineapple pieces with caramel sauce.

Makes about 4 servings

 TIP Be sure to grill pineapple on a very clean grid for the best flavor. It can pick up a bitter taste from the charred bits of burnt food left on the grid.

Grilled Dessert Crumble

1 prepared pie crust
4 slices pineapple
1 large peach or nectarine, cut into 8 wedges
1 large pear, cut into 8 wedges
2 tablespoons sugar
1 teaspoon ground cinnamon
8 ounces whipped topping
4 mint sprigs (optional)

1. Prepare grill for direct cooking.

2. Spray metal pie pan with nonstick cooking spray. Place crust in pan, pressing dough onto bottom and up sides. Grill over medium heat about 14 minutes or until golden brown. Set aside to cool.

3. Spread pineapple, peaches and pear on baking sheet. Combine sugar and cinnamon in small bowl; sprinkle over fruit. Grill fruit over medium heat until golden brown and crisp-tender, turning occasionally. Cut pineapple into bite-size pieces, discarding core. Cool slightly.

4. Break apart crust; divide pieces among four bowls. Top with whipped topping and fruit. Garnish with mint sprigs.

Makes 4 servings

 TIP Firm, almost ripe, fresh fruit holds up best on the grill. Overripe fruit tends to get mushy and soft. Since grilling caramelizes the sugars, slightly underripe fruit turns out sweet and delicious on the grill. For extra sweetness, brush fruit with honey or maple syrup at the end of cooking because sugar burns very quickly.

Grilled Chocolate-Peanut Butter Bananas

1 cup chocolate syrup
¼ cup peanut butter
4 firm bananas, unpeeled
2 tablespoons melted butter
8 tablespoons packed brown sugar, divided
1 pint vanilla ice cream
¼ cup chopped peanuts

1. Heat chocolate syrup in small saucepan over medium heat until warm. Slowly whisk in peanut butter until well blended. Keep warm.

2. Prepare grill for direct cooking. Slice unpeeled bananas in half lengthwise; brush cut sides with melted butter. Grill bananas, buttered side down, over high heat 3 to 4 minutes or until grill marks appear. Turn bananas; spoon 1 tablespoon brown sugar on each banana half. Grill, covered, until brown sugar is melted and bananas have softened.

3. Slide bananas out of their peels with spoon.

4. Place bananas in serving dishes. Place one scoop of ice cream in center. Drizzle with warm chocolate sauce and sprinkle with peanuts. *Makes 4 servings*

 TOOL TIP Grill baskets work well for grilling pieces of fruit and vegetables that you don't want falling through the grid. You can find many other products like grill toppers (metal or wire mesh pans with medium-sized holes) or foil liners with precut slots to place on top of the grill for grilling small or delicate foods.

Chocolate-Caramel S'Mores

12 chocolate wafer cookies or chocolate graham cracker squares
2 tablespoons caramel ice cream topping
6 large marshmallows

1. Prepare grill for direct cooking.

2. Place 6 wafer cookies top side down on plate. Spread 1 teaspoon caramel topping in center of each wafer to within about ¼ inch of edge.

3. Spear 1 to 2 marshmallows onto long skewers or wood-handled fork.* Hold several inches above heat 3 to 5 minutes or until marshmallows are golden and very soft, turning slowly.

4. Push one marshmallow off into center of caramel. Top with plain wafer. Repeat with remaining marshmallows and wafers.

Makes 6 servings

*If wood-handled forks are unavailable, use oven mitt to protect hand from heat.

 TIP S'mores, a favorite campfire treat, got their name because everyone who tasted them wanted "some more." In the unlikely event of leftover s'mores, they can be reheated in the microwave on HIGH 5 to 10 seconds.

Grilled Peaches with Raspberry Sauce

  1 package (10 ounces) frozen raspberries, thawed
1½ teaspoons lemon juice
  3 tablespoons brown sugar
  1 tablespoon rum or water
  1 teaspoon ground cinnamon
  4 medium peaches, peeled, halved and pitted
  2 teaspoons butter
  4 mint sprigs (optional)

1. Combine raspberries and lemon juice in food processor; process until smooth. Refrigerate until ready to serve.

2. Prepare grill for direct cooking.

3. Combine brown sugar, cinnamon and rum in medium bowl; coat peach halves with mixture. Place peach halves, cut sides up, on large sheet of foil. Dot with butter. Double fold sides and ends to seal packet, leaving head space for heat circulation. Grill packet over medium heat 15 minutes. Remove from grill; carefully open end of packet to allow steam to escape.

4. To serve, spoon 2 tablespoons raspberry sauce over each peach half. Garnish with fresh mint sprigs.

Makes 4 servings

Spiced Grilled Bananas

  3 large firm ripe bananas
¼ cup golden raisins
  3 tablespoons packed brown sugar
½ teaspoon ground cinnamon
¼ teaspoon ground nutmeg
¼ teaspoon ground cardamom or coriander
  2 tablespoons butter, cut into 8 pieces
  1 tablespoon lime juice
    Vanilla ice cream or frozen yogurt

1. Spray 9-inch pie pan with nonstick cooking spray. Cut bananas diagonally into ½-inch slices. Arrange, overlapping, in prepared pie plate. Sprinkle with raisins.

2. Prepare grill for direct cooking.

3. Combine brown sugar, cinnamon, nutmeg and cardamom in small bowl; sprinkle over bananas and raisins and dot with butter. Cover pan tightly with foil. Grill, covered, over low heat 10 to 15 minutes.

4. Carefully remove foil and sprinkle with lime juice. Serve over ice cream.

Makes 4 servings

 TOOL TIP Foil pie pans work well in this recipe. Instead of wrapping the pan in foil, cover with the same size pan for a lid.

Acknowledgments

The publisher would like to thank the companies and organizations listed below for the use of their recipes and photographs in this publication.

Alouette® Spreadable Cheese, Alouette® Baby Brie®,
Alouette® Crème de Brie, Chavrie®, Saladena®, Montrachet®

American Lamb Board

Australian Lamb

California Olive Industry

Hillshire Farm®

Holland House® is a registered trademark of Mott's, LLP

MASTERFOODS USA

Mrs. Dash®

National Cattlemen's Beef Association on behalf of The Beef Checkoff

National Honey Board

National Onion Association

National Pork Board

National Turkey Federation

Newman's Own, Inc.®

Reckitt Benckiser Inc.

Reprinted with permission of Sunkist Growers, Inc. All Rights Reserved.

Unilever

Metric Conversion Chart

VOLUME MEASUREMENTS (dry)

$^1/_8$ teaspoon = 0.5 mL
$^1/_4$ teaspoon = 1 mL
$^1/_2$ teaspoon = 2 mL
$^3/_4$ teaspoon = 4 mL
1 teaspoon = 5 mL
1 tablespoon = 15 mL
2 tablespoons = 30 mL
$^1/_4$ cup = 60 mL
$^1/_3$ cup = 75 mL
$^1/_2$ cup = 125 mL
$^2/_3$ cup = 150 mL
$^3/_4$ cup = 175 mL
1 cup = 250 mL
2 cups = 1 pint = 500 mL
3 cups = 750 mL
4 cups = 1 quart = 1 L

VOLUME MEASUREMENTS (fluid)

1 fluid ounce (2 tablespoons) = 30 mL
4 fluid ounces ($^1/_2$ cup) = 125 mL
8 fluid ounces (1 cup) = 250 mL
12 fluid ounces (1$^1/_2$ cups) = 375 mL
16 fluid ounces (2 cups) = 500 mL

WEIGHTS (mass)

$^1/_2$ ounce = 15 g
1 ounce = 30 g
3 ounces = 90 g
4 ounces = 120 g
8 ounces = 225 g
10 ounces = 285 g
12 ounces = 360 g
16 ounces = 1 pound = 450 g

DIMENSIONS

$^1/_{16}$ inch = 2 mm
$^1/_8$ inch = 3 mm
$^1/_4$ inch = 6 mm
$^1/_2$ inch = 1.5 cm
$^3/_4$ inch = 2 cm
1 inch = 2.5 cm

OVEN TEMPERATURES

250°F = 120°C
275°F = 140°C
300°F = 150°C
325°F = 160°C
350°F = 180°C
375°F = 190°C
400°F = 200°C
425°F = 220°C
450°F = 230°C

BAKING PAN SIZES

Utensil	Size in Inches/Quarts	Metric Volume	Size in Centimeters
Baking or Cake Pan (square or rectangular)	8×8×2	2 L	20×20×5
	9×9×2	2.5 L	23×23×5
	12×8×2	3 L	30×20×5
	13×9×2	3.5 L	33×23×5
Loaf Pan	8×4×3	1.5 L	20×10×7
	9×5×3	2 L	23×13×7
Round Layer Cake Pan	8×1½	1.2 L	20×4
	9×1½	1.5 L	23×4
Pie Plate	8×1¼	750 mL	20×3
	9×1¼	1 L	23×3
Baking Dish or Casserole	1 quart	1 L	—
	1½ quarts	1.5 L	—
	2 quarts	2 L	—